Strategic Studies Institute
and
U.S. Army War College Press

THE EVOLUTION OF LOS ZETAS
IN MEXICO AND CENTRAL AMERICA:
SADISM AS AN
INSTRUMENT OF CARTEL WARFARE

George W. Grayson

April 2014

*****

Comments pertaining to this report are invited and should be forwarded to: Director, Strategic Studies Institute and U.S. Army War College Press, U.S. Army War College, 47 Ashburn Drive, Carlisle, PA 17013-5010.

*****

This manuscript was funded by the U.S. Army War College External Research Associates Program. Information on this program is available on our website, *www.StrategicStudies Institute.army.mil*, at the Opportunities tab.

*****

*****

The Strategic Studies Institute and U.S. Army War College Press publishes a monthly email newsletter to update the national security community on the research of our analysts, recent and forthcoming publications, and upcoming conferences sponsored by the Institute. Each newsletter also provides a strategic commentary by one of our research analysts. If you are interested in receiving this newsletter, please subscribe on the SSI website at *www.StrategicStudiesInstitute.army.mil/newsletter*.

FOREWORD

Los Zetas, which appeared on the scene in the late-1990s, have raised the bar for cruelty among Mexican Mafiosi. Traditionally, the country's narcotics cartels maximized earnings by working hand-in-glove with police, military officers, intelligence agencies, union leaders, and office holders affiliated with the Institutional Revolutionary Party (PRI), which dominated the political landscape from 1929 to 2000. An informal set of rules benefited both the drug capos and their allies in government posts. On the one hand, officials raked in generous payments from the malefactors for turning a blind eye to—or employing the Federal Judicial Police and other agencies to facilitate—the growing, storage, processing, and export of marijuana, cocaine, heroin, and methamphetamines.

In return for this treatment, the kingpins were expected to keep their substances away from children, leave civilians (and especially Americans) alone, and limit their arsenals to weapons less powerful than those possessed by the armed forces. Meanwhile, the kingpins only executed enemies in remote areas (preferably north of the Rio Grande), obtained permission from rival big shots before crossing their turfs, and demonstrated respect for mayors, governors, and other prominent figures. Office holders often rubbed elbows with well-known crooks. Nevertheless, should honchos ignore the guidelines or otherwise embarrass the PRI regime, the government would retaliate with shadowy hit squads, executing the rule breakers or consigning them to long prison terms. It should be noted, however, that while incarceration is unpleasant, the "deluxe" prisoners often enjoyed comfortable accommodations and access to vintage wines, female visitors, television sets, and other perquisites denied the average inmate.

Although never functioning with precision, the ad hoc pact system lasted until the late-1970s or even the early-1980s. A series of inept presidents eroded the PRI's sway over society, giving rise to a more transparent society; the 1994 North American Free Trade Agreement multiplied trilateral trade in legal and illegal substances; and the success of the U.S. efforts to stanch the influx of Colombian cocaine into Florida forced the Medellín and Cali cartels to use Central America and Mexico as their major thoroughfare to American consumers. What had once been a multi-million dollar enterprise became a multi-billion dollar venture—a change that further undermined the PRI-government-narco unofficial understanding.

A key figure in this breakdown was Juan García Ábrego, the intrepid chieftain of the Gulf Cartel, centered in Matamoros south of Brownsville, Texas, who pioneered an arrangement with the Colombians whereby Mexican criminals would no longer simply transport cocaine from Central America to the American "big nose," as one pundit expressed it, but take the drugs at the Guatemalan border and assume the risk (and earnings) for transporting the cargo through, around, or over Mexico into the United States. President Ernesto Zedillo (1994-2000) spearheaded the arrest of Juan García Ábrego in 1995, and leadership of the Gulf Cartel wound up in the hands of Osiel "The Friend Killer" Cárdenas Guillén. Osiel's enemies had soared with the paranoid new boss's ascent, and he plied with money, drugs, and better living conditions members of the Airborne Special Forces Groups (GAFEs) to encourage them to desert the army and become his Praetorian Guard against friends and foes he believed were plotting his *coup de grâce*. These hardened, trained killers were Los Zetas, whose name derived from either the police signal used to identify them or the blue zeta color of their uniforms.

Despite Los Zetas' ruthless commitment to The Friend Killer's protection, the military relied on an informant to apprehend Cárdenas in March 2003. At first, the paramilitaries worked in tandem with the new, but inept, honchos of the Gulf Cartel. Yet, gradually Los Zetas charted their own course until they broke with the Gulf syndicate in early-2010. A medley of factors accelerated the schism: (1) the readiness of Los Zetas to enter situational alliances with the Beltrán Leyva Organization, enemies of the mighty Sinaloa Cartel; (2) the botched attempt of the Zeta's second-in-command to import cocaine from Colombia, and, above all, (3) Los Zetas' diabolical cruelty, embellished by their social media's dissemination of beheading, castrations, and unspeakable torture. Briefly speaking, Los Zetas have rewritten the rules of the game to the point that anything goes. Regrettably, other syndicates like the La Familia Michoacán, the Knights Templars, and even the Sinaloa Cartel have copied some of their abominations, giving rise to what Grayson calls the "Zetanization" of Mexico's ineffective drug war.

The author, who has written numerous books and articles on Mexico's underworld, breaks new ground in arguing that the concerted use of sadism has advanced the agenda of a relatively small fist of cutthroats who, despite the elimination of key chiefs, have penetrated a score of Mexican states, inflicted their hideous brand of warfare on Central America, and managed to con-

trol Nuevo Laredo, the largest commercial portal join-
ing Mexico to its northern neighbor.

DOUGLAS C. LOVELACE, JR.
Director
Strategic Studies Institute and
    U.S. Army War College Press

ABOUT THE AUTHOR

GEORGE W. GRAYSON is the Class of 1938 Professor of Government Emeritus at the College of William & Mary, and has made more than 200 research trips to Latin America. In addition, he is a senior associate at the Center for Strategic and International Studies, an associate scholar at the Foreign Policy Research Institute, a board member at the Center for Immigration Studies, a life member of the National Association for the Advancement of Colored People, and a frequent lecturer at the at the U.S. Department of State. He has served as an official observer at six Mexican presidential and gubernatorial elections. He served in the Virginia state legislature for 27 years. He comments frequently on National Public Radio and its affiliated stations. Besides preparing two dozen books and monographs for Center for Strategic and International Studies, Dr. Grayson has authored *The Cartels: the Story of Mexico's Most Dangerous Criminal Organizations and Their Impact on U.S. Security* (Praeger, 2013); *The Impact of President Felipe Calderón's War on Drugs on the Armed Forces: The Prospects for Mexico's "Militarization" and Bilateral Relations* (Strategic Studies Institute, U.S. Army War College, 2012); *The Executioner's Men: Inside Los Zetas, Rouge Soldiers, Criminal Entrepreneurs, and the Shadow State They Created* (co-authored with Sam Logan, Transaction Publishers, 2012); *Threat Posed by Mounting Vigilantism in Mexico* (Strategic Studies Institute, U.S. Army War College, 2011); *La Familia Drug Cartel: Implications for U.S.-Mexican Security* (Strategic Studies Institute, U.S. Army War College, 2010); *Mexico: Narco-Violence and a Failed State?* (Transaction Publishers, 2010); *Mexico's Struggle With Drugs and Thugs* (Foreign Policy Association, 2009); *Mexican Messiah:*

Andrés Manuel López Obrador (Penn State University Press, 2007); *Mesías Mexicano* (Random House-Mondadori, 2006); *Mexico: the Changing of the Guard* (Foreign Policy Association, 2001); *Strange Bedfellows: NATO Marches East* (University Press of America, 1999); *Mexico: From Corporatism to Pluralism?* (Harcourt Brace, 1998); *Oil and Mexican Foreign Policy* (University of Pittsburgh Press, 1988); *The North American Free Trade Agreement: Regional Community and the New World Order* (University Press of America, The Miller Center, University of Virginia, 1995); *The United States and Mexico: Patterns of Influence* (Praeger, 1984); and *The Politics of Mexican Oil* (University of Pittsburgh Press, 1980). His articles have appeared in the *Commonwealh Magazine, Harvard International Review, ForeignPolicy. com, Foreign Policy, Orbis, World Affairs, The Baltimore Sun, The Christian Science Monitor*, the *Houston Chronicle, The Globe and Mail*, the *Los Angeles Times, Newsday, Reforma* (Mexico City), *U-T San Diego, The Washington Post, The Washington Times*, and *The Wall Street Journal*. Dr. Grayson holds a Juris Doctorate from the College of William & Mary and a Ph.D. from the Paul H. Nitze School of Advanced International Studies of Johns Hopkins University.

SUMMARY

The United States has diplomatic relations with 194 independent nations. Of these, none is more important to America than Mexico in terms of trade, investment, tourism, natural resources, migration, energy, and security. In recent years, narco-violence has afflicted our neighbor to the south — with more than 50,000 drug-related murders since 2007 and some 26,000 men, women, and children missing. President Enrique Peña Nieto has tried to divert national attention from the bloodshed through reforms in energy, education, anti-hunger, health care, and other areas. Even though the death rate has declined since the chief executive took office on December 1, 2012, other crimes continue to plague his nation. Members of the business community report continual extortion demands; national oil company Petróleos Mexicanos (PEMEX) suffers widespread theft of oil, gas, explosives, and solvents (with which to prepare methamphetamines); hundreds of Central American migrants have shown up in mass graves; and the public identifies the police with corruption and villainy. A common fear of the elite and growing middle class is kidnapping. In 2012, Mexico recorded 105,000 cases; in 2013, the country led the world in abductions, surpassing such volatile nations as Afghanistan, Colombia, and Iraq.

Los Zetas, who deserted from the army's special forces in the late-1990s, not only traffic in drugs, murder, kidnap, and raid PEMEX installations, but also involve themselves in extortion, human smuggling, torture, money laundering, prostitution, arson, prison breakouts, murder for hire, and other felonies. While consisting of only a few hundred hard core members, these paramilitaries have gained a reputation for the sadistic treatment of foes and friends—a legacy of their two top leaders, Heriberto "The Executioner" Lazcano Lazcano and Miguel Ángel "El 40" Treviño Morales, who thrived on beheadings, castrations, "stewing" their prey in gasoline-filled vats, and other heinous acts. They make sophisticated use of social media and public hangings to display their savagery and cow adversaries.

The reputation for the unspeakable infliction of pain has enabled these desperados to commit atrocities in a score of Mexican states, even as they expend their presence, often in league with local gangs and crime families, in Guatemala, El Salvador, Honduras, and other nations of the Americas. From their bastion in Nuevo Laredo, Mexico, across the border from Laredo, Texas, they also acquire weapons, entrée to legal businesses, and teenage recruits. According to the Federal Bureau of Investigation, the fiends have contracted with such outfits as the Texas Mexican Mafia prison gang, the Houston's Tango Blast, and the McAllen, Texas-based Los Piojos to collect debts, acquire vehicles, carry out hits, and sign up thugs to fight their foes in the Matamoros-centered Gulf Cartel for which Los Zetas originally served as a Praetorian Guard.

Washington policymakers, who overwhelmingly concentrate on Asia and the Mideast, would be well advised to focus on the acute dangers that lie principally south of the Rio Grande, but whose deadly avatars are spilling into our nation.

THE EVOLUTION OF LOS ZETAS IN MEXICO AND CENTRAL AMERICA: SADISM AS AN INSTRUMENT OF CARTEL WARFARE

INTRODUCTION

Drug-related violence in the border town of Nuevo Laredo, the crown jewel for U.S.-Mexican commerce, left the bustling, crime-afflicted city of 350,000 without a police chief. Alejandro Domínguez Coello, a print-shop owner and Chamber of Commerce president, accepted the post on the morning of June 8, 2005. "I'm not beholden to anyone. My commitment is to the citizenry," stated the 56-year-old father of three. Six hours later, he took the wheel of his Ford F-150 pickup. A vehicle pulled up next to him, and the crack of an AR-15 rifle sounded as 30 bullets ripped through his white shirt, splashing blood over his chin and chest. Los Zetas paramilitaries were sending a message: We control the streets of Nuevo Laredo. "They are openly defying the Mexican state," said Mexico City political scientist Jorge Chabat. "They are showing that they can kill anybody at any time. It's chilling."[1]

As a result of such carnage, virtually every other drug trafficking organization (DTO) in Mexico, the more professional law enforcement units, Mexican and U.S. security agencies, and the armed forces are committed to exterminating Los Zetas, who sprang to life in the late-1990s. Osiel "The Friend Killer" Cárdenas Guillén, who aspired to lead the then-mighty Gulf Cartel based in Matamoros across from McAllen, Texas, feared assassination to the point of paranoia. Hooked on cocaine and haunted by internal demons, the 31-year-old Friend Killer became convinced that

1

assassins were plotting his demise. Osiel yearned to rise from a run-of-the-mill boss to a feared capo. Along the way, his climb to the top of the Gulf Cartel brought with it enemies — gangs and individuals who had suffered apace with his ascent — and accentuated his fear of a sudden, ignominious death. Often on a whim, he ordered triggermen to hunt down and execute real and imagined foes. His obsession with being sent to his grave prematurely often "paralyzed" him, according to an astute biographer.[2]

Burdened by the weight of this angst, Osiel had earlier approached military personnel, seeking protection. One of his first contacts was with Lieutenant Antonio Javier Quevedo Guerrero, a former member of the 21st Cavalry Regiment in Nuevo León. After Quevedo's capture on March 29, 2001, Osiel increasingly relied on Lieutenant Arturo Guzmán Decena, who had developed skills in explosives, counterinsurgency, and tracking down and apprehending enemies during his military career.[3]

The delusional boss told Guzmán Decena that he wanted the best men possible. The lieutenant informed the kingpin that they were only in the army and proceeded to help him enlist 31 defectors from the elite Airborne Special Forces Groups, known as GAFEs. The khaki-clothed Benedict Arnolds were seduced by higher salaries — referred to as a "*cañonazo de dólares*" or cannon ball of dollars — compared to the pittance they earned in uniform. Moreover, prominently placed "narco-banners" promised that they would no longer have to eat "Maruchan," a packaged noodle soup, which makes Spam seem like *foie gras*. Still not satisfied with their prowess, Osiel ordered the recruits, then numbering approximately 50, to undergo 2 months of rigorous training in Nuevo León to broaden their skills.

Osiel gave each recruit $3,000, called *la polla* (a pullet or young hen), with which the newcomer could procure cocaine, cross into the United States, find buyers for his merchandise, and then attempt to enlist them as vendors. This artifice acquainted the novices with the petty drug market, broadened their influence into south Texas, and amplified the cartel's distribution network. The military turncoats could reinvest their profits in acquiring more cocaine and multiply their earnings, according to "Rafael," a protected witness. It was said that Heriberto "The Executioner"/"El Lazca" Lazcano Lazcano, who was destined to head the mercenaries, purchased 18 kilograms of the white powder.[4] Guzmán Decena also offered opportunities for rapid advancement. By 2011, after more than a year of fierce fighting with their former masters in the Gulf Cartel, new Zetas could reach the position of hitman in a few months, a process that once took several years, at best. Years later, the capture or killing of several dozen senior Zetas made it possible to rise from skilled shooter to plaza boss more rapidly.

The Gulf Cartel lost a key operative when the army detained Rubén "El Cacahuate"/"The Peanut," the syndicate's treasurer, on November 21, 2002. Four months later, a greater calamity befell the organization. An informer, Second Lieutenant Alejandro Lucio "Z-2," revealed Osiel's whereabouts, and not even Los Zetas could prevent their boss's apprehension in mid-March 2003.

After authorities arrested Cárdenas Guillén on March 14, 2003, Lazcano, renowned as a vicious fighter and strategist, became an ever-more important player, reorganizing Los Zetas into regional cells composed of specialized cadres (*estacas*), lookouts or "falcons," and auditors, who kept tabs on finances where the group held sway. He also sought instruction from deserters from the Guatemalan special forces known as Kaibiles. These "killing machines" are subjected to excruciatingly harsh training in their jungle camps. They must learn to eat "anything that moves," bite the heads off live chickens, and kill puppies after bonding with them. The unit's motto is: "If I advance, follow me. If I stop, urge me on. If I retreat, kill me."[5]

Osiel's arrest left his brother, Ezequiel "Tony Tormenta," Eduardo "El Coss" Costilla Sánchez, and Gregorio "El Goyo" Saucedo Gamboa disoriented and divided over strategy. Meanwhile, the Sinaloa Cartel, led by the redoubtable Joaquín "El Chapo" Guzmán Loera and the Beltrán Leyva Organization (BLO) sought to take advantage of the power vacuum by invading Gulf Cartel areas in the north. Los Zetas distinguished themselves in repulsing the onslaught, and, according to a captured paramilitary, by July 17, 2006, Lazcano had taken control of the outfit. Although not a product of the military as he claimed, Miguel Ángel "El 40" Treviño Morales became No. 2 in the ranks of the upstarts. Los Zetas gradually turned with a vengeance against their master. They entered into situational alliances with the rival BLO, a Sinaloa-founded cartel that had severed ties with the Sinaloa Cartel.

As indicated in Appendix I, the Zeta-Gulf fissure gradually widened, but the break did not occur until early-2010; nevertheless, "El Goyo" Saucedo (arrested on April 29, 2009), "Tony Tormenta" (killed on November 5, 2010), and "El Coss" (captured on September 12, 2010) were businessmen who regarded the grotesque practices relished by Lazcano and Treviño Morales as bad for their sales of cocaine, marijuana, and heroin. Never more than a few hundred cadres,

Los Zetas have suffered scores of losses. The fallen include "The Executioner," whom the navy's marines killed on June 17, 2011, while he was casually dressed and nonchalantly watching a baseball game in Saltillo, Coahuila, apparently without the platoon of body guards that surrounded him on trips to other parts of the country. On July 15, 2013, the marines captured El 40 outside of Nuevo Laredo, Tamaulipas, the citadel of his support. Such setbacks aside, the rogues carry out their venal activities in 21 of 32 Mexican states, have penetrated Central America, and continue to attract recruits. Unconfirmed reports indicate that they are even using West Africa as a springboard to the European market. This monograph argues that, while the key leaders were important, the success enjoyed by the demonic commandos springs from their readiness to use the most heinous forms of violence against their foes.

What explains Los Zetas leaders' behavior, which is characterized by aggressive, manipulative, and demeaning behavior aimed towards others? Abusiveness and violence are common in the sadists' social relationships, because the sadist lacks concern for people and derives pleasure from harming or humiliating others just for pleasure, according to the mental health community, which has labeled such traits as sadistic personality disorder (SPD). Professionals differentiate an individual with SPD from those who are aggressively antisocial inasmuch as the latter typically do not hurt others for pleasure.[6] The comportment of Lazcano and Treviño Morales provides a textbook example of the SPD criteria,[7] which are set forth in Appendix II. A scientific study of their acute misanthropy may appear in the future if psychiatrists, psychologists, and other scientists can gain access to the men's large families and learn the conditions that surrounded their up-bringings. It is known that the late Lazcano was born on December 25, 1974, in Apan, a ramshackle village in Hidalgo famous for producing *pulque*, an alcoholic beverage made from the fermented sap of the maguey plant. He joined the army at age 17, gained promotion to corporal in the infantry in 1993, and was selected for the GAFEs, from which he resigned on March 27, 1998. He acquired several nicknames, including "El Verdugo" or the "The Executioner," because folklore held that he thrived on feeding some of his victims to his private collection of lions and tigers.[8]

Treviño Morales was raised in a poor, dysfunctional family of at least six brothers and six sisters in Nuevo Laredo, Tamaulipas, but the year of his birth is uncertain — with 1970 being the most frequently used (1973, 1976, and 1980 appear in different documents).[9] The skinny young "Miguelito" spent his formative years in Dallas, learned English, and did odd jobs for affluent families, cutting lawns, cleaning chimneys, and washing cars, including one owned by a regional drug dealer who would become a mentor, according to a U.S. Government source.

He abhorred Mexico's de facto caste system, which injected a poisonous sense of inferiority into its disadvantaged citizens. "He always had a chip on his shoulder, which explains his explosive personality," a U.S. law enforcement official said. "He really believed that in Mexico you gain power, respect with brute force."[10] A hitman for Los Zetas later said that El 40 could not sleep at night unless he killed. Treviño Morales loved to hunt, whether his prey was deer or people.[11]

He joined the unscrupulous Los Tejas gang in Nuevo Laredo, spent time in a Dallas jail, and served as a federal policeman in Matamoros before casting his lot with the Gulf Cartel leader. He has a broad network of relatives in the United States – some of whom were involved in criminal pursuits.[12] Not to be considered an American, El 40 had *Hecho en México* (Made in Mexico) tattooed on the back of his neck; the figure of a spitting cobra slithered down his forearm.[13]

A less convincing explanation of Los Zetas' macabre exploits is that they were emulating pre-Colombian human sacrifices by the Mayan and Aztec civilizations. Some of the cadres allegedly seek the good offices of *Santísima Muerte* (The Holy Death), who takes the form of a grim reaper image squeezing a scythe with her bony hand. "The narco-traffickers have always been very religious; they are no atheists," according to University of Nuevo León psychologist José María Infante. "She (*Santísima Muerte*) is a figure who accords with their activities where life and death are closely intertwined," he added.[14] Instruction in decapitations by the Kaibiles, Guatemala's elite jungle squad, may have led Los Zetas to adopt chopping off heads as an important stratagem.[15] Mexico's former Public Security Minister Genaro García Luna insisted that the inspiration for this horrendous tactic was al-Qaeda in Iran, which circulated via the Internet the execution of an Iraqi prisoner.[16] In contrast to his depiction as a demon, El 40 told authorities that he was a farmer with a common-law wife and four children who earned only 40,000 pesos ($3,200) per month.[17]

Without knowing the origin of their unspeakable brutality, 10 factors illuminate how fiendishness advances the organization's objectives: (1) branding; (2) diversifying criminal activities; (3) maximizing extortion and ransom payments; (4) gaining publicity; (5) entering ad hoc alliances; (6) infusing an esprit de corps; (7) successfully recruiting newcomers and lofting to leadership spots these young cadres — often unknown to authorities — who understand that the path to success lies in beheadings, castrations, and immersing foes in vats of boiling grease; (8) discouraging desertions from their ranks; (9) intimidating the weak to commit crimes in a cost-effective manner; and (10) unlike other cartels, using women, known as *panteras*, or panthers, to seduce or kill key politicians, police, and military personnel who can assist Los Zetas. Brief segments will describe activities of the miscreants in the United States, the obstacles they face, and possible steps to combat them.

BRANDING

In 2009, Treviño Morales convened a meeting of crooked police in Nuevo Laredo, a drug-smuggling mecca across the border from Laredo, Texas. No sooner had these law enforcement officers, who constituted 70 to 80 percent of the municipality's force, slouched into their seats when El 40 warned against betraying Los Zetas, Mexico's most potent drug syndicate after the Sinaloa Cartel.

Following this harangue, a brace of thick-necked hoodlums dragged into the dimly lit room a distraught female officer whom El 40 condemned as a government informant. Rather than allowing her to utter a single syllable in her defense, the thugs tied her hands and prevented her from moving. Treviño Morales stepped forward, grabbed a two-by-four, and, after a couple of practice swings as if he were batting clean-up, methodically began to beat her, beginning with her tear-stained face. Once released, the alleged traitor's remains consisted of body fluids, viscera, and splintered bones so mangled, bruised, and bloodied that it was impossible to recognize that she had a few minutes earlier been a sentient human being. The stunned and frightened onlookers got the point.

Los Zetas again acted beyond the pale in the aftermath of the deadly assault on Arturo Beltrán Leyva on December 16, 2009, with whom they were allied. The only marine killed in the protracted firefight was Third Petty Officer Melquisedet Angulo Córdova, who had been buried with honors. The following week, Los Zetas furtively drove to the young man's home in Paraíso, Tabasco, and slaughtered his mother, sister, brother, and aunt.[18] Not even the Sicilian Mafia exacts revenge against the families of fallen military men.

Between April 6 and June 7, 2011, Los Zetas halted several buses that were bound for the border towns of Reynosa and Matamoros, abducted the passengers, and killed some 193 people in what became known as the "Second San Fernando Massacre." There are few journalists in San Fernando; however, unconfirmed reports indicate that the captors forced their prey into gladiatorial blood combat, compelling them to fight to the death with other hostages, complete with hammers, knives, machetes, and clubs, "to find (potential) recruits who were willing to kill for their lives."[19]

In view of such abominations, the White House labeled Los Zetas "a unique and extraordinary threat to the stability of international economies and political systems," comparable to the Camorra secret network in southern Italy, the Yakuza mob in Japan, and the Brothers' Circle of Eastern Europe.[20] The author was cautioned not to even utter the word "Zeta" aloud when walking with a friend in the picturesque streets of Xalapa, Veracruz, a state infested by these bandits. If these paramilitaries seek protection payment from, say, an auto dealer, he knows that failure to comply with their demand will lead to the bombing of his showroom and, very likely, the abduction and fearsome death of a loved one. Among other villainies, they have mastered the preparation of a "guiso" or "stew." The recipe is simple: a child or adult is sliced and diced, his or her blood-soaked body plunged into a pig cooker or rusty 55-gallon oil drum, and doused with gasoline. In some cases, the extent of the destruction caused by this "cook-out" obviates taking reliable DNA samples.[21]

Authorities managed to identify the charred remains of Rodolfo Rincón Taracena, whom the killers abducted in 2007. According to the Committee to Protect Journalists, the seasoned reporter's offense was to have exposed criminals targeting slot-machine patrons at "narco-tiendas" or small stores selling drugs in Villahermosa, Tabasco's capital. The alleged malefactors belonged to a Zeta cell headed by José Akal Sosa.[22] Other acts of brutality include:

- On May 13, 2012, Mexican policemen discovered 49 headless, footless, and handless bodies in Cadereyta, contiguous to Monterrey, on a highway to the U.S. frontier. Although Los Zetas denied committing the atrocity, the culprits sprayed the message "Z 100%" on a wall near where the bodies were found.[23] A week later, authorities arrested Daniel de Jesús "El Loco" Helizondo Ramírez, who said that Treviño Morales had ordered him to get rid of the corpses in Cadereyta.[24]
- On February 19, 2012, Los Zetas staged the Apodaca prison riot, where 44 Gulf Cartel inmates were killed and 37 Zetas escaped;[25]
- On January 4, 2012, Los Zetas ignited the Altamira prison brawl in which 31 Gulf Cartel inmates perished;[26]

- On August 25, 2011, a fist of Los Zetas entered the Casino Royale in Monterrey, ordered everyone out of the building, splashed accelerant on the ground floor, and set the structure ablaze. Fifty-three people died. A police officer, who may have been an accomplice, identified the paramilitaries as the culprits. In retaliation, Zeta gunmen shot the officer's stepfather, stepmother, and brother.[27]
- On May 15, 2011, authorities discovered the bodies of 27 Guatemalan farmers executed by Los Zetas, who were pursuing the campesinos' boss;[28]
- In August 24, 2010, Los Zetas seized 72 Central American and South Americans in San Fernando, a busy crossroads in Tamaulipas state, 85 miles south of the U.S. border. They bound and blindfolded their abductees before shooting them. Mexico's security spokesman Alejandro Poiré Romero said the massacre took place because the migrants either refused to join the cartel or could not pay an extortion fee. Responding to a tip from a survivor, military personnel found the corpses in a ranch building;[29]
- On July 29, 2009, at 5 a.m., two cars stopped in front of the residence of the head of the police in Veracruz, in south-central Mexico. Eight or nine hoodlums jumped from the vehicles and began to fire assault rifles and 40 mm grenade launchers. Within 5 minutes, they had blasted their way into the house, executing Chief Jesús Antonio Romero, his wife, their son, and a police officer. Then they torched the home, incinerating the remaining three children, all girls;[30] and,

- On June 22, 2004, Lazcano masterminded the slaying of the crusading editor of the Tijuana-based weekly newspaper, *Zeta* (no relationship to the criminals), Francisco Javier Ortiz Franco in front of his two children, ages eight and ten. "We consider this a challenge to authority, but also a challenge to Baja California society," stated Governor Eugenio Elorduy Walther. "This is the results (sic) of the efforts that have been undertaken against organized crime."[31]

Guisos, castrations, butchery, skinnings, incinerations, beheadings, and other gruesome practices serve several purposes. They infuse fear in enemies, who often shy from confrontations with these ghoulish desperados; they bolster their chances to extort money from their targets; they gain widespread media attention that generates an ambience of fear and distrust; they dissuade all but the most valiant journalists from covering their deeds; and they send messages to rival cartels. With respect to the last point, security expert Alejandro Hope said: "They are fighting to defend their reputation for brutality and the image of control in the territories they claim."[32]

Such savagery has not always been part of life in Nuevo Laredo or in other criminal enclaves such as Reynosa, Matamoros, Tampico, and Ciudad Victoria in the South Carolina-sized state of Tamaulipas. Decades of neglect, economic malaise, rampant official corruption, and the effect of enormous criminal wealth on an impoverished populace have weakened the government's presence and power in the northeastern shoulder of the country, one of the most dangerous regions in Latin America. (See Map 1.)

Map 1. Tamaulipas.

Entry into Guatemala.

The Zeta brand facilitated their 2007 entrée into Guatemala via the jungle-swathed El Petén, a sparsely populated department, contiguous to Mexico, which is endowed with Tikal and other fabulous Mayan ruins. (See Map 2.) Under the leadership of El 40, they made common cause with prominent, wealthy smuggler Horst Walther "The Tiger" Overdick, who spawned contacts in the nation's labyrinthine under-world from his headquarters in Alta Verapaz.[33] They helped their ally assassinate his strongest adversary, Juan "Juancho" León, who had been stealing from Overdick, even as he charged Overdick fees to cross Juancho's domains.[34] In Cobán, the capital of Alta Verapaz, they confronted the local strongman, Otto Salguero. On May 16, 2011, they traveled to his Los

13

Cocos ranch near the town of Caserio La Bomba in El Petén and relatively close to the Mexico border. There, they encountered some 29 of Salguero's field workers, including two children and two women, most of whom were decapitated and their heads flung helterskelter across the pastures. Local authorities believe that they took the leg of one of their victims and used it to daub a sanguinary message on a wall, reading: "Where is Otto Salguero? You (Salguero) are going to experience what you find here." President Álvaro Colom Caballeros (2008-12) arrived at the scene of the carnage, supposedly to direct the investigation. He declared a state of siege, closed local schools for a day, and detained one suspect.[35]

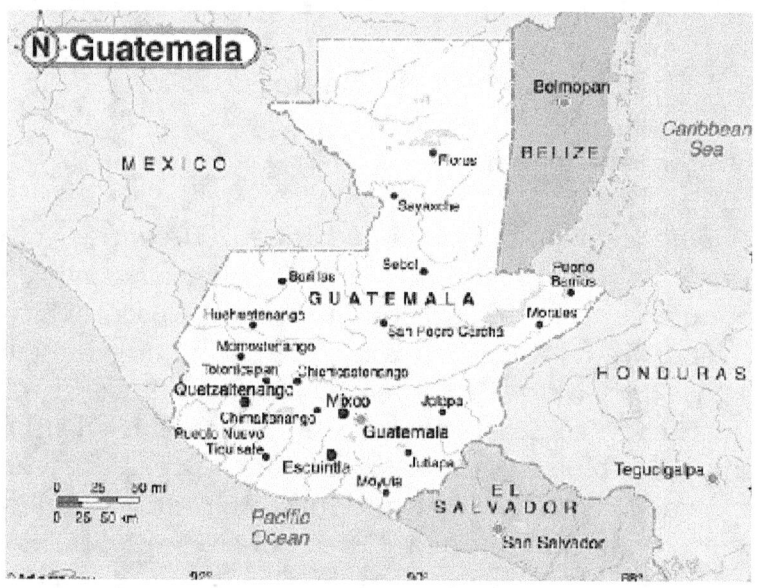

Map 2. Guatemala.

Los Zetas then returned to Cobán, grabbed the son of local official Allan Stowlinsky Vidaurre, and cut him into small pieces. The word was unambiguous: "We control Guatemala."[36] If not a failed state, Guatemala is "a very challenged state with serious institutional deficiencies"[37] that evinces even more corruption than Mexico. Exhibit A of this status springs from the May 19, 2013, action by the nation's Constitutional Court to annul the 80-year sentence for genocide and other crimes against humanity of former retired General José Efraín Ríos Montt. A staunch anti-communist, U.S. Cold War ally, Pentecostal minister, and de facto president (in the early-1980s), he ruthlessly repressed guerrillas during the country's lengthy civil war (1960 to 1996) that took some 200,000 lives, mostly Mayans. A *coup d'état* brought him to the presidency for 2 years (1982-83), during which time he was convicted of ordering the deaths of 1,771 members of the Ixil Maya ethnic group.[38]

Los Zetas established bases in Poptún and Sayaxché in El Petén. Poptún, a zone honeycombed with small roads and clandestine landing strips, borders Belize and is a haven for recruiting cadres. It is also the location of a Kaibiles' training camp referred to as El Infierno (The Hell). Mexican authorities contend that alumni of this facility have aligned with Los Zetas and operate in Mexican territory.[39] Sayaxché, which is relatively close to Mexico and provides ideal smuggling corridors, will eventually connect Alta Veracruz with the nation's west coast by means of the Franja Transversal del Norte (Figure 1, Northern Border Crossing) superhighway now under construction by Israeli contractors. This 221-mile thoroughfare, funded by the Central American Economic Integration Bank at a cost of $240 million, will link the departments of Huehuetenango, Quiché, Alta Verapaz, and Izabal, winding up in Honduras.

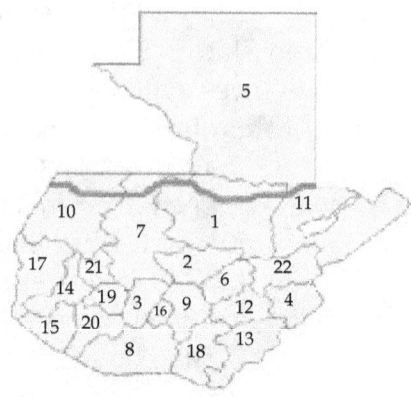

1. Alta Verapaz	9. Guatemala	17. San Marcos
2. Baja Veracruz	10. Huehuetenango	18. Santa Rosa
3. Chimaltenango	11. Izabal	19. Solola
4. Chiquimula	12. Jalapa	20. Suchitepéquez
5. Petén	13. Jutiapa	21. Totonicapán
6. El Progreso	14. Quetzaltenango	22. Zacapa
7. El Quiché	15. Retalhuleu	
8. Escuintla	16. Sacatepéquez	
Source: "Guatemala: Northern Highway Will Start in October," available from *www.centralamericadata.com/en/article/home/Guatemala_Northern_Highway_Will_Start_in_October*.		

Figure 1. Route of Franja Transversal del Norte Superhighway.

The inability to attract sufficient investment facilitated the entry into Central America of criminal elements. The so-called Mexican border with Guatemala resembles a sieve blasted by shotgun pellets, and Los Zetas and the Sinaloa Cartel take advantage of some 300 pedestrian crossings to penetrate their southern neighbor. In 2010, Mexico had only 125 immigration officials to cover their country's 620-mile frontier between the two nations, and leaked U.S. cables indicated that aircraft traveling from Guatemala to Mexico at night had a 100 percent success rate.[40] Its ambassador to Mexico, Fernando Andrade Díaz Durán, lamented that "The Guatemalan government is extremely concerned because during the last 3 or 4 years, Los Zetas have consolidated their presence in all of our country."[41] President Otto Pérez Molina aspires to hold joint maneuvers with Mexico and the United States, which could include posting a brigade at the frontier, especially in San Marcos department.[42] Similarly, Colombia's chief executive Juan Manuel Santos has ordered the Colombian National Police (PNC) to investigate whether Los Zetas are active in his country.

Los Zetas are also ensconced in Zacapa, the capital of an eastern department by the same name and a thoroughfare for importing drugs and other contraband from Honduras and El Salvador. Their presence in several Central American nations aside, Los Zetas have endured their trials and tribulations. In May 2011, President Álvaro Colom announced the capture of ex-Kabil Hugo Álvaro Gómez Vásquez, a Zeta chieftain who reportedly spearheaded the murder of 27 peasants at the Los Cocos ranch; Otto Pérez Molina, elected president in 2011 and promising to brandish an "iron fist" against organized crime, announced the "extremely important" arrest of Overdick on property that he owns outside Guatemala City. Not only was the accused suspected of facilitating the Mexican paramilitaries' move into the north of his country, but he was also wanted in the United States on charges of conspiracy to smuggle cocaine.[43] In March 2012, Guatemala's government announced the capture of Gustavo Adolfo "Comandante Chapoy" Colindres, believed to be a notable local Zeta operator. In February 2013, the nation's security forces apprehended 16 of their countrymen who belonged to La Bomba, a murderous gang linked to Los Zetas. Interior Minister Mauricio López Bonilla explained that 14 people were detained in the southern department of Escuintla and two others in the contiguous department of Guatemala.[44]

In mid-2013, Los Zetas suffered another blow when authorities seized Eduardo "Guayo" Villatoro Cano in Tuxtla Gutiérrez, Chiapas. One of the kingpins in Huehuetenango, Guayo headed a gang that was believed to work with the Mexican cartel. The hunt for Villatoro, which involved hundreds of pursuers, followed the July 2013 slaying of eight policemen and the kidnapping of a PNC agent in the Quetzaltenango's Salcajá municipality.[45]

An additional frustration for Los Zetas took place in early-October 2013 when Guatemalan official Eddy Byron Juárez announced the incarceration of El Yankee, a key Zeta leader in his country.[46] Meanwhile, further to the south in late-2009, bicycle-riding shooters assassinated retired General Julián Arístides González, the Honduran Army's anti-drug czar who was traveling without body guards after dropping his daughter off at school. "Almost all the big Mexican organizations are carving out territory here. And when they run into each other, they will fight over it," González told *Time* magazine before his demise. Officials said they had offered the drug czar bodyguards, but he turned them down. "I would say to him, 'Are you not going to have security?'," his wife said at his funeral. "He replied to me: 'My security is God walking beside me'."[47] The Sinaloa Cartel also has formidable presence in the country.

Honduras is also a strategic transit point where the Mexicans challenge their Colombian, Peruvian, and Venezuelan suppliers over prices and deliveries. San Pedro Sula boasts one of the highest per capita homicide rates in the world, as presented in Appendix V. It wrestled this dubious distinction from Ciudad Juárez. San Pedro Sula came in first in 2013, with Acapulco finishing second, according to Brazilian scholar Jorge Wertheim.[48] Honduran Police Director José Luis Muñoz Licona reported record confiscation of drugs, with Los Zetas believed to be the principal traffickers, representing a monumental adversary that "no nation can take on by itself."[49] Muñoz's bona fides are suspect, as he backed President Porfirio Lobo Sosa's firing of anti-cartel crusader Oscar Álvarez, the nation's security minister. Not only did Álvarez work well with U.S. agencies, but he also publicly demanded that Muñoz Licona fire 10 policemen that he asserted were acting as "air traffic control men" for drug-bearing aircraft.[50]

A ray of good news pierced the black clouds in April 30, 2013, when Rómulo Emiliani, Roman Catholic Bishop of San Pedro Sula, and Adam Blackwell, the ambassador of the Organization of American States for security affairs, brokered a limited truce between the Mara Salvatruchas (MS-13) and their nemesis, the 18th Street gang. The accord crystalized after the two men visited Honduran prisons over a period of 8 months.

Marco, spokesman for the MS-13, promised that the delinquents would stop recruiting as part of the pact but would continue to extort small businesses, bus and taxi drivers, or everyday citizens. "Let's go step by step," Marco said. "First zero crime and zero violence, stop the violence. And to stop the violence that's hurting human beings, we will talk about ways to find alternatives." The two gang leaders who talked with journalists emphasized that so many young men go into the gangs because there are no legitimate jobs or opportunities, and they emphasized the need for work. He called on the government, one of poorest in the Americas, to "help us so our young people learn a trade and don't turn out like us," Marco said. "I want my son to be a doctor or a cameraman, not a gangster."[51] Still, the U.S. State Department reports that as much as 87 percent of all cocaine smuggling flights departing South America first land in Honduras.[52]

Salvadoran officials say that a similar arrangement between the antagonists that began in March 2012 lowered the number of violent deaths about 52 percent in 14 months. Skepticism exists with respect to the gambit in Honduras. "The dynamic of violence in the country goes beyond gangs and reflects the existence of multiple actors that are difficult to pinpoint," said Julieta Castellanos, the National University of Honduras rector whose son and a friend were slain in 2011, allegedly by Honduran police and not gang members.[53] Still, El Salvador is known in Mexican narco-war parlance as "El Caminito" (the little highway), not least because of a convenient U.S.-funded motorway built to encourage trade, which it does, markedly in cocaine. The use of the dollar as currency, combined with the receipt of upwards of $4 billion from Salvadorans living in the United States, makes the Massachusetts-sized nation a money-laundering Eden. The late-2013 discovery of 44 dismembered, bullet-ridden, half-naked victims of the MS-13 and Barrio 18 gangs in a mass grave 12 miles west of San Salvador dashed hopes for a peaceful resolution of the local conflict.

In 2012, Salvadoran authorities happened upon $15 million in cash, buried in barrels in what was believed to be a Zetas training camp. This trove was thought to be only a fraction of their hidden loot. In early-2011, an investigation by Tracy Wilkinson, *Los Angeles Times* Mexico bureau chief, uncovered a major drug trail from Honduras into El Salvador, with cocaine repackaged near Dulce Nombre de María in El Salvador's northern province of Chalatenango, "then trucked across Chalatenango and Santa Ana provinces to Guatemala, virtually unhindered" for transport northward. Businessmen and mayors act as money launderers for the cartels and are on their payrolls. Then-Defense Minister David Munguia Payés cautioned that Los Zetas and other Mexican traffickers were "moving their strategic rear guard to Central America."[54] At least one small community appears to have benefited from the commerce in narcotics. "Dulce Nombre de María, once a sleepy, dusty town, is now a sparkling burg," wrote Wilkinson. "The gazebo in the main square is painted in salmon and lavender and decorated with Corinthian columns. Grounds are well manicured, free of beggars and stray dogs. The ice cream vendor wears Ralph Lauren."[55]

In late-August 2012, Mexican narco-financial manipulations became a cause célébré in Nicaragua after its National Police stopped six vans, all emblazoned with the logo of the Mexican media giant TELEVISA, at the Las Manos border crossing with Nicaragua. The 18 Mexican passengers brandished press credentials, top-of-the-line cameras, microphones, cables, a satellite dish, and paper adorned with corporate letterhead. Yet, no volcano had erupted; no hurricane had been spotted; and no election was on tap. Why was the largest Spanish language network in the world sending a convoy through Nicaragua? During a 2-day investigation, the law enforcement officers discovered that the foreigners were criminals, not journalists, and they had $9.2 million stuffed in black gym bags under the floorboards of three vehicles. The *Southern Pulse* newsletter asserted that the suspects had links to Los Zetas, who continually vie with the Sinaloa Cartel for north-south corridors. In any case, observers concluded that the funds were destined for Costa Rica to pay for a shipment of cocaine. Raquel "La Licenciada" Alatorre Correa, leader of the phony journalists, had crossed into Costa Rica 15 times since 2006, although it was unclear whether she had used convoys then. "We were not investigating them," said Costa Rican vice minister of security Celso Gamboa Sánchez. "We were not very shrewd."[56] So even picturesque Costa Rica, bereft of an army, a paradise for environmentalists, and known as the "Switzerland of Central America," appears on the cartels' radar screens.

To curb organized crime in Central America, Guatemalan President Pérez Molina announced, after a meeting with Pope Benedict XVI in the Vatican, that Guatemalan, Mexican, and U.S. forces would fortify the Mexican-Guatemalan border. Among other steps, he would dispatch police and army motorized units to focus on the frontier between San Marcos department and Chiapas. He did not comment on the roles that Mexico and the United States would play in trying to deter movement across what is more a surveyor's line than a clear border.[57] Although any joint action at the frontier remained vague, *InfoSurHoy* reported that Dominican Republic, U.S., and Guatemalan counternarcotics forces seized more than 998 kilograms of cocaine worth upward of U.S.$90 million in the eastern Pacific in early-March 2013. The newspaper referred to "The interdiction [as] . . . another success scored under Operation Martillo, a regional counter-narcotics mission that brings together U.S., Latin American and European countries to cut the flow of illicit drugs through Central America."[58]

In late-2013, it was alleged that pressure on DTOs in Latin America had spurred Los Zetas, the Sinaloa Cartel, and other narco-traffickers to establish maritime drug routes to ports in 16 West African nations and, from there, ship their products to Europe by vehicles and small airplanes.[59] The Sinaloa Cartel has a vastly larger international footprint.

DIVERSIFICATION

Osiel Cárdenas gave Los Zetas small amounts of drugs to sell but never enmeshed them in the narcotics business, much less introduced them to either his major Andean suppliers or prime distributors in the United States. The 11.7-ton container load of cocaine captured in Altamira, Tamaulipas, on October 5, 2007, was intended for El 40. Although eight of his heavily armed cohorts were apprehended, Treviño Morales fled when he realized that law enforcement officials were on the scene. The commandos also move marijuana, harvested mainly in Tamaulipas, and limited quantities of cocaine and heroin to the north.

In addition to drug commerce, Los Zetas was involved in many other activities. As presented in Appendix III, these include extortion, murder for hire, kidnapping, human smuggling, dealing in contraband, petroleum theft, money laundering, prostitution, arson, sale of body parts, car bombing, automobile and truck hijacking, loan-sharking, paying small farmers to grow poppies, running protection rackets, taxing rivals who want to cross their territory (*derecho de plaza*), gunrunning, and stealing gasoline from the aging pipelines of PEMEX, the state oil monopoly. Petroleum specialists, probably from PEMEX's incredibly corrupt union, aid and abet the so-called oil and rustling—a crime that involved 2,167 thefts in 3 years, at a cost of 5,125 million pesos (U.S.$427 million dollars) between 2007 and mid-2012. Although the Gulf Cartel may be involved, the principal culprits are Los Zetas. These cutthroats have also acquired from complicit PEMEX personnel large quantities of explosives, as well as such strong solvents as xylene and toluene, which are destined for hydraulic fracking but which the malefactors use to cook methamphetamine consumed in the United States. The largest robberies have taken place in PEMEX installations in Villahermosa, Ciudad del Carmen, Veracruz, Poza Rica, and Reynosa. The energy reform, approved in 2013, may exacerbate this headache when the volume of detonation materials and specialized chemicals increases as outside companies make direct investments in the nation's hydrocarbon field.

Coal has become another attractive energy commodity. These robberies are creating a "Parallel PEMEX," in the words of an astute journalist.[60] Los Zetas have a stronghold in Coahuila, a state abounding in Zetas that produces 95 percent of the 15 million tons of coal extracted each year. The newspaper *Reforma* reported that the cartel mines or buys 10,000 tons per year. At $50 per ton, the business may generate $22 to $25 million annually.[61]

Not only do they capture and abuse adults caught in their web, Los Zetas also apprehend young girls and boys, whom they exploit sexually or require to work for them. "With minors . . . (they engage) in sexual

24

exploitation, forced labor, slave-like practices, forced marriages, fraudulent adoptions, and the harvesting of (body) organs," according to El Salvadoran prosecutor for illegal trafficking Smirna Salazar de Calles. When young women have babies, they are taken to Guatemala to be sold.[62]

Before the takedown of The Executioner and El 40, Ralph Reyes, Drug Enforcement Administration (DEA) chief for Mexico and Central America, said that Los Zetas were imposing de facto taxes on major corporations. And, while still engaging in atrocities, the cartel has evolved from a militaristic chain of command to "a business structure, with quarterly meetings, business ledgers, even votes on key assassinations."[63] Loss of key personnel has shattered this corporate configuration.

MAXIMIZING EXTORTION AND RANSOM PAYMENTS

Their penchant for obscene cruelty invests Los Zetas with "cartel cred" or credibility in the underworld. For example, failure to make a ransom payment means that the evil doers will return your loved one either without body parts or tortured beyond recognition. A few years ago, Los Zetas exhibited more rational procedures. In 2008, they seized an affluent attorney near the port of Veracruz and held him for 3 days while his son and partners raised the $300,000 demanded for his release. State leaders who learned of the transaction beseeched the lawyer and his family to keep mum about the incident, lest its revelation cast negative publicity on Veracruz, whose governor — like so many of his colleagues — aspired to become Mexico's president one day. Even worse, the state executive allegedly was closely associated with Los Zetas, according to former members of his administration who are now ensconced in a witness protection program. President Calderón even accused outgoing governor Fidel Herrera Beltrán of "leaving the state in the hands of Los Zetas. . . ."[64] Rumors filled the air that the former state executive would receive an ambassadorship, possibly to Greece. Senator Fernando Yunes Márquez, a member of Mexico's National Action Party, expressed opposition to such an appointment on the grounds that the former governor, who had saddled his state with a debt of 50 billion pesos ($4 billion), was under investigation by U.S. authorities for having received millions of pesos from Los Zetas.[65]

Kidnapping cases invariably involve a certain degree of bargaining, even with Los Zetas. In what currency do you want the danegeld? Where do we drop off the money? When do we get our family member back? In the course of these interactions, the brother of the abductee asked: How do we know that once our family member is returned, you will not kidnap him or a sibling next week? Los Zetas' interlocutor assured his counterpart that not only would they pledge not to capture another member of the family or a close friend, but they would also guarantee that no other cartel would take advantage of him. The problem with the "warranty" concept lies in changes in plaza bosses. A new, inexperienced chief is unlikely to adhere to such a code of conduct.

GAINING NOTORIETY

In their ability to attract attention, Los Zetas put Madison Avenue to shame. Occasionally one victim was decapitated, which used to make national headlines. Now a single beheading may only make local news. To ensure broad print and electronic media coverage, these agents of Satan behead multiple enemies and arrange their bodies in a way convenient for TV camera operators and newspaper photographers. In December 2008, Los Zetas captured and executed eight army officers and enlisted men in Guerrero, a violence-torn, impoverished southern state where "triple sovereignty" exists among the inept elected government, narco-criminals, and the violent, anarchistic National Coordination of Educational Workers (CNTE) known as La Coordinadora—with self-defense groups often lashing out at foes. Pictures of the decapitated cadavers lying side-by-side flashed around the world on television and YouTube.

In February 2009, the paramilitaries killed retired Brigadier General Mauro Enrique Tello Quiñones, whom the mayor of Cancún had hired to form a special weapons and tactics (SWAT) team to fight such criminals. They smashed his arms and legs before driving him into the jungle and executing him.[66]

Los Zetas don't hesitate to execute the celebrities who offend them. Artists who cater to one criminal group risk revenge from its enemies. A case in point is Valentín "El Gallo de Oro" Elizalde. The scoundrels gunned down the "Golden Rooster," along with his manager and driver, in an ambush that followed a late-November 2006 concert in Reynosa. The assassins presumably struck because the 27-year old superstar had sung *A mis Enemigos* (To My Enemies), which supposedly represented an anti-Zeta taunt paid for by El Chapo Guzmán and his Sinaloa Cartel. A video showing the execution of a Zeta and the corpse of Tijuana Cartel leader Ramón Arellano Félix accompanied the music.[67] Elements of the Mexican Army and the Attorney General's Office arrested Raúl "El Flander I" Hernández Barrón, one of the original Zetas, for the murder. His brother, Víctor Manuel "El Flander II" had been captured with Osiel on March 14, 2003, in Matamoros. Also suspected in the killing of Elizalde was another Zeta, Raúl Alberto "El Alvín" Trejo Benavides.

The *Arizona Daily Star* reported the death of Sergio Gómez, 34, founder of the popular group K-Paz de la Sierra, which featured fast-paced drums and brass horns. A Chicago resident, Gómez disregarded warnings not to perform in his native state of Michoacán before being abducted and murdered. The same week, gangsters shot and killed Zayda Peña of *Zayda y Los Culpables* (Zayda and the Guilty) in a hospital in Matamoros.[68] Samuel González Ruiz, former chief of a federal organized crime unit, said:

> The cartels don't care about how they are seen by the public, they are worried about showing their absolute control of their territory, and they will impose their control at all costs . . . (killing a singer) is like planting the flag of their cartel in the ground.[69]

González Ruiz also explained how different kinds of murders convey messages to opponents. He claims that a bullet to the temple signifies that the victim belonged to a rival gang, while a gunshot to the back of the head may indicate that the target was a traitor.[70] Narco-lore has it that castrating a man and sewing his genitals in his mouth indicates that he informed on the ogres.

Mayhem, such as killing 72 northbound migrants with sledgehammers in Tamaulipas in 2010, thrusts Los Zetas into the limelight. They disseminate their propaganda via narco-banners draped at urban intersections, broadcasts on their partially disabled radio network, and presentations on social media. Like other criminal bands, they are likely to scrutinize Google, Facebook, Twitter, and Craig's List entries to facilitate the seizure of victims.[71]

Occasionally, though, they try to ingratiate themselves to the public and throw their adversaries off stride. Mexicans celebrate "Children's Day" on April 30. Before this event in 2011, the paramilitaries appeared in a parade in Ciudad Victoria, the capital of Tamaulipas, publicizing a free party at the municipal stadium, complete with gifts for children. Youngsters and parents flocked to the ballpark and joyfully received free food, soft drinks, candy, remote-controlled cars, and upscale bicycles. Before the end of the festivities, organizers unfurled a banner that advised parents to love their children and spend time with them — under the signature of Heriberto Lazcano Lazcano and the Zeta Company.[72] Los Zetas also took advantage of the slow reaction of the Tamaulipas government to the devastation caused by October 2013 Hurricane Ingrid. Near schools in badly afflicted neighborhoods of Ciudad Victoria, the opportunistic desperados purportedly distributed canned and non-perishable food packed in bags marked with the letter Z. The Gulf Cartel, which is engaged in a no-holds-barred battle with the paramilitaries for supremacy in the area, undertook similar actions.[73]

SITUATIONAL ALLIANCES

Los Zetas go out of their way to preserve their independence, which allows them to react quickly to changing circumstances. The Casino Royale fire in Monterrey marked a tectonic shift in the drive to eradicate Los Zetas—with a possible "Showdown at the OK Corral" erupting in southern Tamaulipas and northern Veracruz. The culprits suffered scores of casualties, but they caught authorities and the Sinaloa Cartel off guard when they moved into Sinaloa and Jalisco. In return for Los Zetas' sharing their diabolical *modus operandi*, the Beltrán Leyva Organization has provided money and facilitated their access to Sinaloa, El Chapo's home base. The BLO also helped them make common cause with the Mazatlecos, a gang in Mazatlán, Sinaloa. They have followed the same exchange with La Resistencia, a violent gang that has given them access to Jalisco. El Chapo's confidant, Ignacio "El Nacho" Coronel Villarreal, had dominated the state and, above all, its capital, Guadalajara. He was known as the "King of Crystal" for spearheading crystal methamphetamine output and trafficking until the army killed him on July 29, 2010. Now Los Zetas, aligned with La Resistencia, are important players in Mexico's third largest city, known as the "Pearl of the West" by residents and a money-laundering paradise for narco-traffickers.

ESPRIT DE CORPS

After a withering gun battle, the Mexican marines, an arm of the navy, killed Lazcano in Progreso, Coahuila, in a pre-dawn raid on October 7, 2012. What ensued is worthy of a best-selling "Who done it?" After forensic experts examined Lazcano's corpse, the marines, believing they had gunned down a common criminal, left the capo's remains in a private funeral home in Sabinas, Coahuila, 80 miles from the U.S. border. A day after the takedown, a gang of masked, heavily armed hoods burst into the parlor, overpowered the staff, shoved Lazcano's decaying body into a hearse, and forced the owner to drive to a yet-to-be-discovered venue. What explains this gruesome deed? As ruthless as they are, veteran Zetas sometimes adhere to the tradition, begun by the U.S. Marines in 1775, of never leaving a fallen brother behind, especially if he is a big shot in their hierarchy.

In what became known as the "Invasion of the Body Snatchers," in early-March 2007, Zeta gunmen broke into a cemetery in Poza Rica, Veracruz, used hammers to smash open the gravestone of their comrade, Roberto Carlos Carmona, and carried off the casket containing his cadaver. Gunmen had perforated Carmona with bullets during a clandestine, high stakes horse race in Villarín, near the port of Veracruz.[74]

Los Zetas find other ways to honor their dead. Three months after the army killed Arturo Guzmán Decena, the lieutenant who recruited many of the original deserters, a funeral wreath and four flower arrangements appeared at his gravesite with the inscription: "We will always keep you in our hearts: from your family, Los Zetas." It has been reported that, like the pharaohs of ancient Egypt, Lazcano had an elaborate sarcophagus built for him in his hometown, Apan, Hidalgo, near the site where Los Zetas remodeled an aging chapel. An illuminated, giant silver cross welcomes visitors to the brick sepulcher, which is adorned with stained glass windows and is Christian in character. He had a chapel constructed nearby in honor of his mother.[75] Some observers questioned whether the Zeta boss had been taken down. The Mexican navy indicated that a fingerprint match revealed that Lazcano had been killed. To squelch rumors that El Lazca was alive and well, his family agreed to have the body of his father and other relatives exhumed from a cemetery in Pachuca to carry out a DNA analysis. Although it was announced that the tests corroborated earlier findings, unidentified DEA officials still voiced misgivings about the capo's demise based on the discrepancy between the height of corpse that went missing (5'3") and the U.S. agency's records (5'8"). Local forensics experts also questioned the adequacy of the DNA results.[76]

In addition, Los Zetas spearhead prison breakouts to free their comrades. An especially brazen escape happened in Zacatecas on May 16, 2009, and all of it is available for public viewing on YouTube. Before dawn, 30 or more heavily armed thugs believed to be Zetas, riding in trucks adorned with Federal Investigative Agency (which had replaced the Mexican Federal Judicial police) police logos, stormed into the Cieneguillas penitentiary as one of their helicopters whirred overhead. In the blitzkrieg assault, they extricated 53 prisoners, including Zetas, Beltrán Leyva crime family members, and other narco-felons. State and federal authorities immediately began apprehending escapees even as they investigated the director and his 50 subordinates to determine who fostered the escape. One of several recaptured was Osvaldo "The Vampire" García Delgado, a kidnapping specialist whose Los Cotorros gang coordinates activities with Los Zetas in the state of Hidalgo.

In October 2009, Los Zetas precipitated a riot in the Topo Chico prison in Nuevo León that the state police had to put down. Some 100 Zetas virtually controlled the 400 other inmates in the facility through extortion and by requiring them to pay bribes for protection. Before the uprising, PRI Governor Natividad González Parás had brushed off friction in the penitentiary as: "A squabble between one group of friends against another group of friends over personal problems."[77]

The military defectors even have their favorite *corrido*, ("La Escolta Suicida," or The Suicide Escort), which emphasizes pride in defending their "patron":[78]

We are 20 the group of Los Zetas	*Somos 20 el grupo de Los Zetas/*
United as a family/	*unidos como familia/*
We are 20 the force/	*los 20 somos la fuerza/*
With diplomas of suicide/	*con diplomas de suicida/*
Aware that in each action/	*conscientes de que en cada acción/*
We can lose our life. . .	*podemos perder la vida. . . .*

As in other facilities, Los Zetas practice virtual self-governance in the federal prison in Apodaca, Nuevo León (Cereso), where they attack members of the Gulf Cartel and other foes.

Just as city governments may sponsor book fairs, concerts, film fests, and other cultural activities, Los Zetas take a profound interest in the entertainment events — generally in a negative light. They follow narcocorridos, the ballads sung by vocalists and played by bands that not only venerate drug lords but also provide a form of popular "musical newspaper."

Until recently, Zeta leaders, like corporate chief executive officers, threw annual end-of-the-year parties for their plaza chiefs and senior personnel around the country. These bacchanalias featured culinary delicacies, free-flowing drugs, a harem of high-end prostitutes, drunken song fests, the conferral of bonuses, the possible reassignment of plaza bosses and sicarios, and crates of alcoholic beverages. Whether the revelers drank "Los Zetas" brandy, which comes in a Z-shaped bottle and is sold in Cancún, Solidaridad, and other municipalities in Quintana Roo, is not known.[79] Some Zetas wore uniforms with the markings of their organization; others rejoiced in being awarded medals for their achievements.

SUCCESS IN RECRUITING AND PROMOTING NEW CADRES

Unemployment haunts Mexico. The official joblessness stood at 4.73 percent in February 2014 — down from 4.86 percent in April 2012.[80] If true, this number would be the lowest of all members of the Organization of Economic Development and Cooperation members. The problem is that the figure is pure fiction inasmuch as the government considers an individual to be employed if he works several hours during an entire week. Below are the criteria, roughly translated from the law, on what constitutes employment:

> Persons who during the reference week did any kind of economic activity, being in any of the following situations: Working at least an hour or a day, to produce goods and/or services independently or subordinate, with or without pay. Temporarily absent from work without interrupting their employment relationship with the economic unit. Includes primary sector employees engaged in production for own consumption (except firewood collection). [81]

More important is the informal economy in a country where, amid the growth of a middle class, poverty stalks one-third of its 116.2 million citizens. As a result, 35 percent[82] or more of men, women, and children provide services as day workers; wash car windows at urban intersections of urban streets; hawk baseball hats, videos, books, sunglasses, gaudy jewelry, and other items (many of which are contraband) from folding tables and blankets along the streets of cities and towns; and engage in other pursuits. Economists can only estimate these "off the books" transactions. Los Zetas often coerce these hucksters to serve as lookouts, while their teenage children may become low-level recruits. Scholar John J. Bailey has astutely emphasized the linkage between the underground economy and organized crime.[83] Figure 2 indicates the percentage of the population doing informal work in the 15 states with the lowest number of full-time jobs.

State	Percent Workforce in Underground Economy	Level of Presence of Los Zetas
Oaxaca	80.5	Medium-low
Guerrero	79.2	Low
Chiapas	78.1	Medium-low
Hidalgo	74.3	High
Puebla	74.2	Medium-low
Tlaxcala	73.4	Low
Michoacán	71.6	Low (Except in Lázaro Cárdenas)
Veracruz	67.3	Medium
Morelos	66.5	Low
Zacatecas	65.8	High
Yucatán	64.9	Low
Nayarit	64.1	Low
Campeche	62.5	Medium-low
Guanajuato	62.5	Medium
Tabasco	61.2	Medium

Source: Jorge Ramos, "Agobian informales a los estados pobres; 15 entidades superan la media nacional," Excélsior, May 14, 2013; based on calculations of the Instituto Nacional de Estadística y Geografía (National Institute of Statistics and Geography); the states in which Los Zetas have the strongest presence are Tamaulipas, Nuevo León, San Luis Potosí, parts of Veracruz, and Coahuila (especially Piedras Negras).

Figure 2. Percentage of Workforce in Underground Economy and Los Zetas' Presence in 15 States with High Joblessness.

If youngsters can make several hundred dollars a month, they are willing to cast their lot with the underworld. The paramilitaries also appeal to their cultural preferences. El 40's favorite musical group is Sinaloan-based Banda El Recodo, founded in 1938, which plays *banda* and *ranchera* songs that emphasize love, patriotism, nature, and the achievements of Los Zetas.[84] He realizes that young people resonate more to hip hop than to the traditional corridos. As a result, Los Zetas encourage the playing of a new genre of music, which is very similar to the gangsta rap from the 1990s. In Reynosa and Matamoros, musicians like Cano&Blunt, *Grupo Nektar* (whose leader is believed to be an operative of the CDG, the letters connoting the Gulf Cartel's alliance with the Sinaloa Cartel), and Lyric Dog sing about cartel lieutenants, the organizations' weapons, money, women, and power.

At the same time, there is panache to either working with or being inducted into the leanest, meanest, and most despised criminal outfit in the Americas. The prospect of having a few grams of cocaine, expensive leather boots, access to a fast car, a pistol tucked in your waistband, and the admiration of young women makes young people — the "Ni-Nis" mentioned previously — adhere to the belief that it is better to live like a king for 5 years than to be a burro all your life. Los Zetas exhibit a cockiness or swag less obvious in other syndicates that, on average, have older members. An example involves Rosalio Reta, a young American, whom Los Zetas trained for 6 months in Mexico. He committed his first murder at age 13. During his interrogation, he told the police: "I loved doing it. Killing that first person, I loved it. I thought I was Superman." U.S. officials have said there are many more youngsters like him.[85] As a result, Los Zetas attract teenagers, which they often use as cannon fodder in confrontations with the hostile cartels, the military, and civilian law enforcement agencies.

DISCOURAGING DESERTIONS

There is an adage that "you have to kill to become a Zeta, and you must die to leave Los Zetas." Truth be told, militants have defected from the paramilitaries, leaving behind, of course, their money, cell phones, weapons, and other possessions. A Zeta may succeed in leaving, but his family risks beastly punishment or death. Such retribution is possible because of the records kept by the organization. Figure 3 epitomizes the meticulous bookkeeping precision practiced by one plaza in 1 month.

Expenditures	Amount (In Dollars)	Percentage of Total
Administration of Lookouts	18,400	2.85
Security	1,100	.17
Gifts	50,000	7.73
Raffles (Five Rolex Watches)	25,000	3.86
Payoffs to Police	552,350	85.39
TOTAL	**646,850**	**100.00**

Source: Confidential.

Figure 3. January-September 2007 Expenditures by Los Zetas' Monterrey Plaza.

Almost as bad as fleeing the cartel is emulating its activities. Los Zetas are quick to take revenge on copycats. Above all, they do not want amateurs taking a slice of their market. In addition, the ersatz Zetas, also called "McZetas," may not carry out threats, thus diminishing the credibility of the genuine organization. In October 2007, Zeta imposters demanded first $1 million and then one million pesos from a restaurant owner. Although the pretenders shot up the façade of his home, no one was injured and the family quickly moved to another state.[86] In May 2008, a 35-year-old man was found in Monterrey. He had been tortured, an ice pick plunged through his throat—with a note dangling in his stone cold hand: "This is one of those who carried out extortions by telephone trying to pass for 'Z'."[87]

In February 2009, the goons executed two "false Zetas" in Reynosa, leaving behind a handwritten note saying, "This is what will happen to those who attempt to pass themselves off as Zetas."[88] Although the chances are zero that they will modify their image, real Zetas do not suffer gladly amateurs who try to grab for a slice of their market. Some Zeta plaza bosses will leave a family alone after it cooperates and pays the ransom or extortion money demanded. In contrast, phony Zetas may take repeated actions against the same business or household.

Ersatz Zetas threatened to capture the Spanish musical group Delorean, which flew to Mexico City in early-October 2013 to take part in an electronic music and film festival. An anonymous caller said that Los Zetas would kill the performers if they refused to fork over five million pesos (approximately $385,000). This gambit turned out to be a "virtual kidnapping," which may have been attempted by prison inmates who have access to cell phones and telephone directories.

Several days later, the Anti-Kidnapping Unit of Spain's Guardia Civil rushed to Mexico to protect a Catalonian businessman who, as it turned out, was also the victim of a virtual kidnapping, this time in Querétaro, 137 miles north of the capital. The operation took only 20 hours and frustrated the payment of more than $80,000 demanded by the imposters.[89]

A gang of kidnappers who falsely called themselves Zetas to collect payola in Nuevo Laredo landed behind bars and were promptly murdered. A municipal official said the killings were "most likely carried out on orders from the Zetas." He added that: "The Zetas don't like their names used in vain, plus they want to tell society, 'Hey, we've changed. We're not kidnappers or extortionists. We're one of you'."[90]

COST EFFECTIVENESS

Los Zetas rely on newspaper sellers, street vendors, prostitutes, taxicab drivers, vagrants, and other denizens of city streets, parks, and alleys to serve as couriers and lookouts, which makes even more eyes available to signal threats to their overlords. In addition to spotting the paramilitary's opponents, small merchants may also have to pay few pesos a day for their own protection. Criminals also retain bank tellers, who inform Los Zetas and other cartels about the balances, credit card numbers, ATM accounts, and withdrawals of their clients.[91] The American Express headquarters on Mexico City's Avenida Patiotismo resembles an armed citadel because of the sizeable financial transactions that take place there.

El 40 believed that small-time drug sellers who worked for his organization had skimmed cash they were supposed to turn over to a collection agent. Accompanied by several thugs, the Zeta honcho barged into the boarding house where the vendors lived. The intruders lined the men up against the wall. Then, the Zeta strongman ferociously wielded a two-by-four, pummeling the first alleged cheat to death. The second experienced an even gorier fate. Treviño Morales slashed his throat with a razor-sharp butcher's knife, plunged his hand through the victim's bloody thorax, and yanked out his heart. Los Zetas demand every peso they believe owed to them. "Now Lazcano was a brutal task master and extremely violent," said Mike Vigil, former DEA chief of international operations. "However, Miguel Treviño is 100 percent more violent that Lazcano ever was."[92]

To save resources, Los Zetas contract out work to such lethal gangs as the Barrio Azteca, the Texas syndicate, MS-13, and the remnants of the Carrillo Fuentes and Beltrán Leyva organizations. They also collaborate with smaller drug trafficking groups in Guatemala, Colombia, and Venezuela.[93] Invaluable confederates in Guatemala are Los Chulamicos, who provide weapons, intelligence, safe houses, shooters, and vehicles, and work in concert with the bodyguards of Horst Overdick.

In view of the paramilitaries' blood lust, it is unclear whether they take advantage of paid hitmen in the Hidalgo municipalities of Jacala and Huejutla in central-eastern Mexico, where killing for hire constitutes a long-standing service industry. The Federal Bureau of Investigation (FBI) reports that Los Tolles serve as debt collectors for Los Zetas in Acapulco and facilitate cocaine distribution in Atlanta and other U.S. cities.[94] Los Zetas save money by requiring their employees to turn in expense vouchers to a financial operator, often a woman, who also receives the daily income. Subject to unannounced audits, she bypasses plaza bosses and dispatches the resources to Omar "El 42" Treviño Morales, who assumed leadership of the syndicate after his brother's capture. In addition, low level sicarios stay in fleabag hotels for the sake of economy; they may also sleep in their vans to save money and hide from authorities. In late-October 2011, the navy captured Carmen del Consuelo "Claudia" Sáenz Márquez in Córdoba, Veracruz. Under the supervision of regional leader Raúl Lucio "El Lucky" Hernández Lechuga, whom authorities arrested 2 months later, the 29-year-old blond and her 10 assistants allegedly supervised Zeta finances in Hidalgo, Oaxaca, Tabasco, Quintana Roo, and Veracruz.[95] She received earnings from drug sales, oil thefts, extortion, kidnapping, contraband deals, and other crimes. Claudia used these funds to pay the salaries of regional chiefs, plaza bosses, gunmen, lookouts, and accountants. Furthermore, she purchased communications equipment, bribed officials, and paid off providers of technical services.[96]

FEMALE KILLERS

Sexism pervades Los Zetas, as it does throughout organized crime and other Mexican institutions. El Lazca and El 40 were attracted to busty blonds, some of whom reportedly came from Eastern Europe. Still, with few exceptions, women who have reached leadership roles did so after husbands, brothers, or boyfriends disappeared from the scene. As mentioned earlier, the paramilitaries have a female unit known as the *Panteras*.[97] The task of these Panthers is to negotiate deals with police, politicians, military officers, and others who can assist the deadly outfit. These distaff criminals alter their makeup and the color and style of their hair according to their assignments. They show no compunction about committing grisly executions. Should sex, alcohol, drugs, and pillow talk not elicit the desired outcome, these women may kill the unsuspecting mark. First identified at a party thrown by Lazcano in December 2006, the initial leader of the group—Ashly "La Comandante Bombón"/"The Candy Commander" Narro López—was captured in Cancún on February 9, 2009, in connection with the murder of General Tello Quiñones. Panthers are concentrated in Tamaulipas, Coahuila, and Nuevo León—with jefas in most states.

Women also serve in other areas of Los Zetas' deteriorating structure. On September 11, 2011, the navy apprehended Verónica Mireya Moreno Carreón, 35, also known as "La Vero" or "La Flaka." The ex-police officer assumed the commandos' leadership in San Nicolás de Los Garza, a city in the Monterrey metropolitan area, after the August arrest of her supposed lover, Raúl "El Sureño"/"The Southerner" García Rodríguez. The captors found in her car a 38-caliber revolver, six cell phones, and dozens of envelopes containing cocaine and marijuana.[98]

Rosa Nelly "La Pato" Rodríguez Martínez was an especially vicious distaff Zeta leader in the Monterrey area. A police officer from 2002 to 2008, she took a maternity leave and went over to the dark side. Not only did she hustle drugs in 30 small establishments, but also she allegedly executed five young "chapulines" or "grass-hoppers" who attempted to defect from the organization. She was caught with four presumed members of her cell, including her 31-year-old sister, Ana "La Güera"/"Blondie" Rodríguez Martínez. Their belongings included an AK-47 rifle, six boxes of munitions, 35 grams of marijuana, and 150 psychotropic tablets.[99]

In October 2011, authorities took into custody Nancy "La Flaca" Quintanar Manríquez, 25, in Ecatepec, a huge city contiguous to the Federal District. Her technique was to drop into bars and nightclubs, extract information from Zeta enemies, and have them killed by hitmen such as Julio Caesar "Mosco" Sosa Asencio, 30, who was arrested with her. She is credited with having participated in at least a dozen homicides.[100] Also detained in October 2011 was her 31-year-old sister, Carmen del Consuelo "Claudia" Sáenz.

When arrested in June 2011 after a ferocious firefight involving the paramilitaries in Guadalajara, 16-year-old Maria Celeste proudly told reporters that "I am a shooter at the service of Los Zetas." She claimed to have received training in the use of AK-15s, AR-15s, and other firearms. A teenager like María Celeste earned $305 a week for protecting the cartel's turf and upwards of $1,525 for killing rival mobsters.[101]

On August 21, 2013, the army took into custody Helga Ruth Vázquez Ruiz, a National Action Party member of the Ciudad Victoria city council. A search of a residence belonging to the 44-year-old lawyer turned up 20 million pesos in funds apparently belonging to Los Zetas. The feisty politician, who had a history of clashing with party leaders, claimed that she was the object of political persecution.[102]

In the words of Professor Jorge Chabat, a researcher at the prestigious Center of Investigation and Economic Education: "Narco-trafficking is no longer exclusively for men. Women now take part directly in crimes and also assume (leadership roles)." They work as plaza bosses, mediators, shooters, administrators, and interlocutors. The upshot is that they constitute 5 percent of the country's 221,000 inmates in federal prisons—up from 3 percent in 2006.[103]

The presence of women in the Zeta camp is a mixed blessing. In 2004, El 40 purchased an automobile for his girlfriend, San Juana Ericka Sánchez, from a dealership where Salvador Alfonso "La Ardilla" Martínez Escobedo worked. The couple broke up, and La Ardilla, who was believed to have authored the massacre of hundreds of migrants in San Fernando, wed Sánchez in 2005. The marriage outraged the insanely jealous El 40, who attended the ceremony where he danced inappropriately with the bride. Their cheek-to-cheek, alcohol-induced flirting infuriated the bridegroom and impelled a nasty rupture between Treviño Morales and one of Las Zetas' ranking regional leaders, who was arrested on October 8, 2012.[104]

The hot-tempered El 40 had run-ins with other Zetas that ultimately resulted in his downfall. In addition to La Ardilla, he crossed swords with Iván "El 50"/"El Talibán" Velázquez Caballero, who managed an important network in San Luis Potosí, Zacatecas, Coahuila, Aguascalientes, and Guanajuato. A protected witness said that Treviño Morales, who ousted his brother, Daniel "El Dany"/"El Talibán 2" Velázquez Caballero, from the Durango plaza in November 2008, sought to drive El Talibán from his lucrative holdings. El Talibán reportedly accused El 40 of being a "Judas of Los Zetas" and killed 14 of Treviño Morales' triggermen in San Luis Potosí on August 9, 2012. Within 48 hours, 73 murders took place in San Luis Potosí, Zacatecas, and Monterrey. Iván escaped from these massacres, only to be captured by the marines on September 26, 2012.[105]

Morris Panner, a former Assistant U.S. Attorney who is a senior adviser at the Center for International Criminal Justice at Harvard Law School, learned from informants the breadth of the networks of the Mexican cartels. "Mexican organized crime groups have morphed from drug trafficking organizations into something new and far more dangerous," Mr. Panner said:

> "The Zetas now are active in extortion, human trafficking, money laundering, and increasingly, anything a violent criminal organization can do to make money, whether in Mexico, Guatemala or, it appears, the U.S."[106]

Zeta Incursions into the United States.

- **Activities in Southeast and Midwest**. On October 2, 2008, the FBI's Knoxville Criminal Investigative Division indicated that Los Zetas were carrying out extortion, kidnapping, and drug trafficking in the Midwest and Southeast, with emphasis on East Tennessee, Georgia, and Oklahoma. A detainee told agents that the focus was often on non-Americans who owed money to Zeta leaders, as well as competitors of the paramilitaries' human smuggling undertakings. The same source indicated that Gaspar González Alcantar and Martín "Zeta 21" were involved in these activities.[107]
- **Falcon Dam Incident**. On September 30, 2010, David Michael Hartley, a U.S. citizen, was presumably shot by Zetas during a trip to the Mexican side of the binational reservoir. Los Zetas may have mistaken him for a spy of the rival Gulf Cartel, according to the report by STRATFOR, an Austin-based think tank specializing in intelligence and international affairs. Harley's body has never been discovered, and Mexico's chief investigator for the case, Rolando Flores

Villegas was decapitated — his head delivered in a suitcase to a military post near the Texas border.[108]

- **Recruitment of Gang-Bangers**. Los Zetas seek out children/teenagers inside the United States to accomplish their goals. On April 2006, Laredo detective Roberto Garcia arrested teenager Gabriel Cardona, whom Los Zetas had recruited as a triggerman and all-purpose thug. He stabbed and tortured his victims and put their blood in a glass to toast Santísima Muerte, whose tattoo he sported. He and fellow Texan Rosalio "Bart" Reta, also an American citizen and Santísima Muerte devotee, lived in safe houses in upper-class Laredo. They waited for El 40 or another top Zeta to summon them to action. They worked on both sides of the frontier, allegedly receiving two kilos of cocaine and $10,000 for each assassination. A well-executed hit might yield a bonus of a top-of-the-line Mercedes. The amazing fact about Rosalio Reta is that, after 6 months of military training in Mexico, he was sent across the border to target rival drug gangs. He was only 13 years old when he delivered his first *coup de grâce*.[109]

- **Killing Americans in Mexico.** On February 15, 2011, Los Zetas shot to death Jaime J. Zapata, a U.S. Immigration and Customs Enforcement (ICE) agent who was driving an armored SUV with diplomatic license tags on a Federal Highway 57 in San Luis Potosí, a state infested with Los Zetas. His companion, agent Victor Avila, escaped with a gunshot wound. On March 13, 2010, a U.S. employee of the American consulate in Ciudad Juárez, her husband, and a Mexican linked to the consulate died when drug gang members fired on their cars near the Santa Fe International Bridge in Ciudad Juárez after they left a children's party in El Paso, Texas. Authorities did not tie Los Zetas to this tragedy.[110] However, Zeta Héctor Raúl "El Tori" Luna Luna confessed to participating in the grenade attack on the U.S. Consulate General in Monterrey on October 12, 2008. He claimed to have been acting under the orders of Sigifredo "El Canicón"/"The Marble" Najera Talamantes, who was already under arrest.[111] Between October 2002 and December 2012, 684 American citizens died in Mexico — 40 percent of American violent deaths worldwide in this period. Some of casualties may have been connected with drug activities; most experienced what the Pentagon euphemistically calls "collateral damage."[112]

- **Horse Buying and Breeding.** In May 2012, authorities apprehended José, the younger brother of Miguel Ángel Treviño, who had acquired some 379 quarter horses with drug earnings. Tremor Enterprises LLC served as the front for the purchases, which were made with cash and the use of false names. Most of the horses, which the Internal Revenue Service (IRS) auctioned off, were stabled at a ranch near Lexington, Oklahoma, just south of Oklahoma City. In a show of chutzpah, some of the animals carried names related to the narcotics trade, like Coronita Cartel or the Small Crown Cartel. "This case is a prime example of the ability of Mexican drug cartels to establish footholds in legitimate U.S. industries and highlights the serious threat money laundering causes to our financial system," according to Richard Weber, the chief of the IRS criminal investigation unit.[113]

- **Training camp in Texas?** The FBI reported that Los Zetas were training on a ranch in a remote part of Texas. The instruction centered on "neutralizing" U.S. competitors. The FBI also claimed that the brigands protected shipments of cocaine and heroin bound for Houston, where it was packaged and dispatched to destinations in Alabama, Georgia, and Michigan.[114]
- **Arms Purchases.** In early-July 2011, authorities captured Zeta founder Jesús "El Mamito" Rejón Aguilar, who told Mexico's Federal Police that his cartel acquired "all of its weapons" in the United States. It once relied on border crossing points, but now its allies in the United States send them across the Rio Grande. He said it was easier for the rival Matamoros-based Gulf Cartel to bring arms through check points in car trunks, possibly because they have a pact with authorities.[115]
- **Narco-Corridos.** On April 25, 2013, singer Jesús "Chuy" Quintanilla, best known for his ballads extolling the bravado of Los Zetas, was shot two or more times in the head. Farmworkers picking grapefruit found the corpse floating in a pool of his own blood north of Mission, Texas. His songs not only showed "respect" for Los Zetas, but he also had dedicated one to ranking Zeta plaza boss "El Hummer" González Durán, who was captured in November 2008 in Reynosa. Authorities are unsure whether dissident Zetas committed the assassination or gunmen for the Gulf Cartel.[116]

- **Sanctuary Cities**. Mayors of U.S. border cities point with pride to relatively low levels of violence in their municipalities compared with the bloodshed across the Rio Grande. The professionalism of law enforcement agencies is undoubtedly higher, the culture different, and the economy better in the United States. The relative safety in, say, El Paso, means that public officials may work in Ciudad Juárez during the day but cross the river at night to stay in safe lodging. Los Zetas and other cartels also use El Paso and other American twin cities as sanctuaries where they can house their families and pursue youngsters for their exploits. In the 1970s and 1980s, several Mexican cities were like no-fly zones; that is, there was a tacit agreement among criminal organizations not to attack each other or each other's families in these locales; examples were Guadalajara, Morelia, Monterrey, and Mexico City. Now, only Mexico City, Querétaro, and possibly Mérida, bear the characteristics of safe havens.

The late-May 2013 kidnapping of 11 teenagers and young adults from the Heaven After nightclub, a few blocks from the U.S. embassy, has raised concerns about safety in the Zona Rosa tourist center and nearby neighborhoods. The abductions took place in the aftermath of the May 9 murder of Malcolm Shabazz, Malcolm X's grandson, in nightclub in the vicinity of Garibaldi Plaza, a seedy area where tourists come to hear mariachi music. More than likely, the criminals belonged to gangs, not cartels, which frequent the dangerous Tepito market area.[117] In late-December 2013, 10 Zetas raided four residences, including that of controversial journalist Anabel Hernández in Naucalpan, a mega-city contiguous to the Mexican federal district (DF). The unpredictability of violence in the nation amplifies the attractiveness of American border communities. Appendix IV provides a comparison of homicides in the twin cities.

Possible Steps Against Los Zetas and Prospects for the Paramilitaries.

- Although the concept sounded attractive during the PRI candidate's successful presidential race, the creation of a 40,000-member Gendamería Nacional modeled on the eponymous French institution remains in limbo. The use of the military, especially the navy and marines, will be indispensable until the Peña Nieto government configures a new strategy. The Mexicans should be encouraged to look for crime fighting assistance from countries other than the United States. As described earlier in the monograph, agents of the Spanish Guardia Nacional required only 20 hours to protect a Catalonian businessmen from being victimized by a virtual kidnapping in Querétaro.
- Calderón employed the broadsword; that is, sending large contingents of military personnel and Federal Police to go against cartels and their cells. As discussed, the kingpin strategy proved counterproductive. The current administration must rely more on the scalpel, which means eavesdropping, voice detection, DNA profiling, fingerprint analysis, aerial surveillance, and infiltrating Los Zetas and other cartels — with attractive female informants being especially effective.

- In the same vein, it is imperative for U.S. Armed Forces and intelligence agencies to hack into Los Zetas' sophisticated communications networks, sharing information exclusively with vetted Mexican authorities and only if Mexican authorities once again allow their U.S. counterparts access to intelligence gathering fusion centers. Meanwhile, appropriate U.S. agencies should offer to share anti-hacking technology with the Mexican government in view of the widespread sale of databases by the nation's largest banks (Banamex, BBV, Bancomer, HSBC, Santander, American Express) and the Federal Electoral Institute *(Instituto Nacional Electoral)*. In May 2012, Mexico's extremely professional transparency institute *(Instituto Federal de Acceso a la Información y Protección de Datos)* urged the Mexican Attorney General *(Procuraduría General de la República* or PGR)to investigate the security of personal information about citizens.[118]
- Another approach involves even closer cooperation in thwarting money laundering through actions of Mexico's Finance Ministry's Financial Intelligence Unit *(Unidad de Inteligencia Financiera* [UIF]) and the U.S. Treasury Department's Office of Foreign Asset Control (OFAC). With a staff of 100 to 120, UIF issues excellent reports about irregular, unorthodox, and possibly illegal activities by banks, *casas de cambio* (exchange houses), and other financial institutions. For instance, this agency turned over evidence to the Attorney General's Office about the obscenely large amount of resources manipulated by Elba Esther "La Maestra" Gordillo, head of

the venal 1.2-million member *Sindicato Nacional de Trabajadores de la Educacion* (SNTE) Teachers' Union. The PGR charged the woman, once referred to as "Jimmy Hoffa in a skirt," with embezzling $200 million in union funds.[119] Still, the Financial Action Group of South America, created to combat money laundering, indicates that UIF's studies are underutilized by Mexican authorities.[120]

- The National Banking and Stock Commission (*Comisión Nacional Bancaria y de Valores*), which oversees money laundering, must continue to broaden its reach to banks outside major cities, making unannounced inspections of their records. In addition, working through Mexico's astute ambassador in Washington, Eduardo Medina Mora, and the highly experienced financial attaché, José Martín García, the appropriate U.S. officials might suggest considering a modest amendment to Mexico's money-laundering statute,[121] published on October 17, 2012, which allows hotels, resorts, nightclubs, and other border tourism centers to deposit up to $14,000 in cash per month. This limit should be lowered if substantial money laundering appears to be taking place in the particular city or municipality.

- To combat money laundering, U.S. authorities should follow the activities of the late Treviño Morales favorite performers such as Banda El Recodo, which plays on both sides of the border and receives payments as high as $250,000.[122]

- As was the case with Osiel Cárdenas Guillén, the erstwhile leader of the Gulf Cartel who is now serving an abbreviated sentence for information provided about Los Zetas, U.S. and Mexican authorities should be prepared to negotiate fewer years behind bars for extradited Zetas — such as aging founders — who are prepared to furnish details about the leadership, organization, resources, allies, and other elements of the paramilitaries and other crime syndicates.

- The continued use of unmanned aerial vehicles or drones, which helped track down installations of La Familia Michoacána, is imperative. Global Hawk drones can survey areas as large as 40,000 square miles.[123] However, in view of the robust nationalism exhibited by the Institutional Revolutionary Party, U.S. agencies must treat the Mexicans with kid gloves in the deployment of spy planes.

- One of Peña Nieto's biggest challenges is the nation's 31 governors, who rule their states like feudal barons — either shutting their eyes to criminality or actively reaping rewards from drug trafficking. Corruption is endemic, and these state executives are not going to turn into candidates for sainthood. Yet, the president and Finance Secretary Luis Videgaray Caso can use the budget as a carrot or stick to gain cooperation against the underworld. This tool is especially important because states received upwards of 90 percent of their funds from Congress. If the state executives prove intransigent, the president can eschew making much-coveted visits to their bailiwicks and refuse to recommend their states to foreign investors.

- An important element in reducing the tsunami of violence that washed over Ciudad Juárez was the involvement of the business community, religious leaders, the U.S. Government through the Mérida Initiative, local officials, and nongovernmental organizations in what was known as *Todos Somos Juárez*. This venture gave rise to the lighting of soccer fields, the creation of youth baseball leagues, the formation of musical groups, and scores of activities for citizens, especially young people. By the beginning of 2013, the murder rate had fallen 90 percent from its high point in late-2010. Such a civic venture could help reduce the influence of Los Zetas in the commercial portal of Nuevo Laredo, where murders shot up 92.5 percent from the 2012 level, even as kidnappings have soared.[124]
- Cartels take advantage of lax juvenile laws in Mexico and the United States. States should be encouraged to prosecute family members whose children are involved in commercial drug trafficking. The age should also be lowered for the prosecution of youthful offenders who knowingly aid and abet the drug trade for criminal organizations.[125]
- PEMEX must enhance its deployment of drones, satellites, and trucks with detector devices to impede the robbery of hydrocarbons from pipelines.[126] Sales of oil and natural gas account for one-third of the nation's budget at a time that, without substantial new investment, Mexico will become a net hydrocarbon importer by 2020, according to respected analysts.[127] In addition to hydrocarbon thefts, Los Zetas (and

the Gulf Cartel, to a lesser extent) are stealing large quantities of explosives from PEMEX, as well as such potent solvents as xylene and toluene to help cook methamphetamines. The rogues often substitute water for the chemicals, which—when used in hydraulic fracking—permanently damage the rock formations at the bottom of a well and decrease the additional oil and gas that can be extracted. Authorities should examine raw materials recovered from Zeta sites to determine the proprietary chemical compounds used in its production process.

- The corruption of teachers' unions such as SNTE and CNTE produces unemployed, uneducated youngsters—the so-called "Ni-Nis"—whom Los Zetas and other syndicates welcome into their ranks. Mexico's 2013 educational reform is unlikely, at least in the short- to medium-term, to break the hammerlock that venal teacher organizations have on public education. The United States should condition aid for community development on the introduction of vouchers to Mexican parents, so they can decide the schools in which they wish to enroll their children.

- In off-the-record conversations, private contractors working with Mexican security agencies deplore the mismanagement, waste, and corruption infusing the Attorney General's Office and other law enforcement arms of the Mexican government. U.S. legislators and officials who oversee the disbursement of monies should demand regular, unannounced audits by independent firms of Mexican beneficiaries of this assistance.

- Los Zetas and other cartels have penetrated the U.S. Department of Homeland Security and the Border Patrol. It is imperative that personnel and sister agencies undergo thorough background and polygraph tests before they assume their responsibilities along the border and that periodic checks take place if and when they are hired.
- The fall of Lazcano and Treviño Morales proved a sharp thorn in the side but not a lethal dagger to the heart of Los Zetas. The marauders have managed to dominate Nuevo Laredo amid attacks by the Sinaloa and Gulf Cartels, as well as by the Federal Police, the armed forces, and U.S. agencies. The commandos are bereft of the command and control structure they once enjoyed, to the point that expert Ioan Grillo depicts many of new leaders as directing self-financing "orphan cells" that operate on a free-lance basis. In late-December 2013, Mexico's Attorney General's Office averred that of the 69 capos brought down by the Peña Nieto regime, Los Zetas sustained the most arrests (23) and killings (4). Still, venality allows the miscreants also to rank high among cartels in terms of spilling blood, accomplishing kidnappings, and garnering money. They may be masters of sadism, but they are not effective businessmen. For instance, as early as 2008, El Lazca reportedly began to share, and later delegate, the designation and oversight of plaza bosses to El 40, who had developed his own contacts with Colombian cocaine suppliers. The latter practiced meritocracy and set rigid earnings objectives. When operators fell short of these goals,

the latter-day Simon Legree unceremoniously embarrassed, demoted, or replaced them. Such clashes suggest the wisdom for U.S. and Mexican officials funneling, sub rosa, intelligence about intramural conflicts to the Gulf and Sinaloa cartels to exacerbate ruptures among the paramilitaries.

- Unlike their business-oriented rivals, Los Zetas have not acquired real estate and other assets to give them alternative sources of revenue. This argues for an increased budget for OFAC, which has done a first-rate job of not only seizing Zeta-owned properties in El Norte, but also helping to discovering triangular linkages among the cartel's illegal activities in the United States. A case in point was the money laundering that involved Francisco Antonio Colorado Cessa, head of ADT Petroservicios, S.A., who was a PEMEX contractor at the same time he was heavily doing the bidding of Los Zetas.[128]

- U.S. officials dealing with DTOs that operate in Mexico and the United States must remember that the Mexican officials—even more so than their foreign counterparts—are prone to believe that amending the Mexican Constitution, enacting a statute, or signing a pact means that a problem is solved. In fact, formal rituals frequently trump serious changes in behavior.[129]

ENDNOTES

1. Quoted in "Border-town Killing Sends Message," *Los Angeles Times*, June 10, 2005, in George W. Grayson, "Los Zetas: The Ruthless Army Spawned by a Mexican Drug Cartel," *E-Notes*, Philadelphia, PA: Foreign Policy Research Institute, May 2008.

2. Ricardo Ravelo, *Osiel: Vida y tragedia de un capo* (*Osiel: Life and Tragedy of a Capo*), Mexico City, Mexico: Grijalbo, 2009, pp. 172-175.

3. *Ibid.*

4. "Invierten' sicarios en cartel" ("Triggermen 'Invest' in Cartel"), *El Nuevo Heraldo*, March 1, 2010.

5. Tracy A. Bailey, "Ranger Graduates Kaibil School," *ShadowSpear Special Operations*, December 18, 2012, available from *www.shadowspear.com/2012/12/army-ranger-graduates-kaibil-school/*.

6. "Sadistic Personality Disorder Criteria," *Psychnet-UK*, March 2013, available from *www.psychnet-uk.com/x_new_site/ personality_psychology/a_diagnostic_criteria/criteria_personality_ sadistic.html*.

7. See George W. Grayson and Samuel Logan, *The Executioner's Men: Los Zetas, Rogue Soldiers, Criminal Entrepreneurs, and the Shadow State They Created*, New Brunswick, NJ: Transaction Publishers, 2012.

8. Tracy Wilkinson, "Top Drug Cartel Leader in Mexico Possibly Killed in Firefight, Officials Say," *Los Angeles Times*, October 8, 2012.

9. "Requiere Estados Unidos al 'Z-40'" ("The United States Request 'Z-40,'"), *Reforma*, July 16, 2013.

10. Dianne Solís and Alfredo Corchado, "Top Leader of Mexico's Zeta Group Has Dallas Roots," *Dallas News*, April 13, 2013, updated July 17, 2013.

11. The comments of Rosalio Reta appear in Jason Buch, "Trevino Morales had Nasty Itch for Killing, ex-Gang Member Says," *San Antonio Express-News*, July 17, 2013.

12. "New Cartel Leader Violent 'to the Point of Sadism'," *ABC Radio News*, October 12, 2012. For the names and ages of his siblings and mother, see Anabel Hernández, "Life, Times, and Tragedies of the Treviño Clan," *Borderland Beat*, October 27, 2012 (this article was translated from the October 27, 2012, edition of *Proceso*).

13. "Asegura Z-40 ser un agricultor" ("Z-40 Asserts that He Was a Farmer"), *Reforma*, October 14, 2013.

14. "El culto de Santísima Muerte, un boom en México" ("The Cult of the Holy Death Is Booming in Mexico"), *Terra*, available from *www.terra.com/arte/articulo/html/art9442.htm*.

15. Will Grant, "Mexico Violence: Fear and Intimidation," *BBC News* (Latin America and Caribbean), May 14, 2012.

16. Ioan Grillo, "Behind Mexico's Wave of Beheadings," *Time* magazine (World Ed.), September 8, 2008.

17. "Asegura Z-40 ser un agricultor."

18. Roberto Barboza Sosa, "Zetas y policías asesinos de familia de marino" ("Zetas and Police Assassinate Family of Marine"), *El Universal*, December 23, 2009.

19. Dane Schiller, "Mexican Crook: Gangsters Arrange Fights to Death of Entertainment," *Houston Chronicle*, June 11, 2011; and "Invasion of the Body Snatchers," *Reuters*, March 9, 2007.

20. Stephen Braun, "President Obama Levels Executive Order at Zetas, Yakuza, Camorra and the Brothers' Circle" (video), *Huffington Post*, July 25, 2011; and J. Jaime Hernández, "Obama: 'Zetas,' global threat," *El Universal*, July 26, 2011.

21. "Mexico's Violent Zetas Cartel sees New Leader Emerge," *Fox News Latino*, August 23, 2012.

22. "Mexican Journalist Dismembered, Burned, Officials Say," *CNN World*, March 1, 2010.

23. Jo Tuckman, "Mexican Drug Cartel Massacres Have Method in Their Brutal Madness," *The Guardian*, May 14, 2012.

24. "The Eerie Logic of the Zetas Cartel's Most Infamous Actions," *ABC News Univisión*, October 10, 2012.

25. "Official: Guards Aided Zetas Prison Break," *CBS News*, February 20, 2012.

26. "Police Detain 20 in Mexican Prison Riot," *Fox News*, January 5, 2012.

27. Nick Valencia, "Police: Killing of 3 Look Like Revenge for Mexico Casino Massacre," *CNNWorld*, September 15, 2011.

28. Ken Ellingwood and Alex Renderos, "Massacre Leaves 27 Dead in Northern Guatemala," *Los Angeles Times*, May 15, 2011.

29. Dudley Althaus, "Seven Arrested in Mexico Massacre," *Houston Chronicle*, September 8, 2010.

30. Michael Ware, "Los Zetas Called Mexico's Most Dangerous Drug Cartel," *CNN.com/world*, August 6, 2009.

31. Anna Cearley and Sandra Dibble, "Tijuana Newspaper Editor Shot to Death," *UT-San Diego*, June 23, 2004.

32. Quoted in Tuckman, "Mexican Drug Cartel Massacres Have Method in Their Brutal Madness."

33. "El capturado Z-40 organizó a los Zetas en Guatemala" ("The Captured Z-40 Organized Los Zetas in Guatemala"), *El Universal*, July 18, 2013.

34. *Ibid.*

35. Moisés Castillo, "Guatemala Hunts for Killers of 27 on Ranch," *UT-San Diego*, May 17, 2011.

36. Steven Dudley, "Guatemala: cuando llegaron 'Los Zetas'" ("Guatemala: When 'Los Zetas' Arrived"), *Proceso,* September 22, 2011.

37. James Derham, American ambassador to Guatemala, 2005-2008; e-mail to author, June 2, 2013.

38. Sam Logan, "Guatemala: Ríos Montt's 80-year Sentence Annulled," *Southern Pulse,* May 28, 2013; and "Guatemala's Rio Montt Found Guilty of Genocide," *BBC News* (Latin America and Caribbean), May 10, 2013.

39. "Álvaro Colom anucia captura de lider de Los Zetas en Guatemala" ("Álvaro Colom Announces Capture of Zeta Leader in Guatemala"), *El Universal,* May 18, 2011.

40. Pablo Ordaz, "Narcos y contrabandistas toman la frontera sur de México" ("Narco-traffickers and Contraband Smugglers Take Mexico's Southern Frontier"), *El País (International),* December 11, 2010.

41. "Crecen Zetas en frontera sur" ("Los Zetas Grow in Southern Border"), *Reforma,* February 17, 2013.

42. Irene Savio, "Anuncia Guatemala operativo con México" ("Guatemala Announces Operation with Mexico"), *Reforma,* February 17, 2013.

43. "Guatemala Drugs: Zetas Cartel Suspect Overdick Arrested," *BBC News* (Latin America and Caribbean), April 3, 2012.

44. "Capturan a 16 guatemaltecos supuestamente vinculados con Los Zetas" ("16 Guatemalans Supposedly Linked to Los Zetas Captured"), *EFE,* February 07, 2013.

45. "How Salcaja Massacre Tests Guatemala's Resolve," *In SightCrime,* September 17, 2013.

46. "Confirman captura de presunto jefe de los Zetas" ("Arrest of Presumed Zeta Chieftain"), *Publinews,* October 12, 2013.

47. Mariela Rosario, "Honduran Drug Czar Murdered," *Latina,* December 21, 2009.

48. Jorge Werthein, "Cuáles son las 20 ciudades más violentas del mundo" ("What are the World's 20 Most Violent Cities"), November 30, 2013, available from *jorgewerthein.blogspot.com/2013/11/cuales-son-las-20-ciudades-mas_30.html*.

49. Quoted in Iris Amador, "Los Zetas Sows Fear While Expanding Reach Throughout Central America," *Diálogo*, October 17, 2011.

50. Geoffrey Ramsey, "Honduran Security Minister Steps Down, Deepening Security Crisis," *Christian Science Monitor* (Latin America), September 13, 2011.

51. The quotations in this section appeared in Alberto Arce, "Honduran Gangs Declare Truce, Ask Talks with Gov't," *Associated Press*, May 28, 2013.

52. Bureau of International Narcotics and Law Enforcement Affairs (INCSR), "2013 INCSR: Country Reports — Honduras through Mexico," Washington, DC: U.S. Department of State, March 5, 2013.

53. Alberto Arce, "Honduran Gangs Declare Truce, Ask Talks with Gov't," *Associated Press*, May 28, 2013.

54. Tracy Wilkinson, "El Salvador Becomes Drug Traffickers' 'Little Pathway'," *Los Angeles Times*, March 22, 2011.

55. *Ibid.*

56. Quoted in Adriana Gómez Lincón, "Big Cash Seizure Puts Light on Nicaragua Drug Role," *Associated Press*, August 31, 2012.

57. Irene Savio, "Anuncia Guatemala operative con México" ("Guatemalan Operation with Mexico Announced"), *Reforma*, February 17, 2013.

58. Ezra Fieser, "Operation Martillo: More than 600 Pounds of Cocaine Seized," *Infosur Hoy*, January 22, 2013.

59. The countries mentioned are Benin, Burkina Faso, Cape Verde, Côte d'Ivoire, Gambia, Ghana, Guinea, Guinea Bissau,

Liberia, Mali, Mauritania, Niger, Nigeria, Senegal, Togo, and Sierra Leone; see Julieta Pelcastre, "Los Zetas Smuggles Drugs to Europe through West Africa," *Inforsurhoy.com*, October 11, 2013. While the international role of Los Zetas is dubious, U.S. security experts agree that the Sinaloa Cartel has a much more extensive web of global connections.

60. Noé Cruz Serrano, "Robo financie un paralelo'" ("Robberies Have Financed a 'Parallel PEMEX'") *El Universal*, July 31, 2009.

61. "El carbón, nuevo lucrativo negocio para el cartel mexicano de Los Zetas" ("Coal, a New Lucrative Business for Los Zetas Cartel"), *El Universal*, November 25, 2012.

62. José Meléndez, "Opera narco mexicano trata infantil" ("Mexican Narcos Smuggle Young Children"), *El Universal*, May 5, 2013.

63. Quoted in Ware, "Los Zetas Called Mexico's Most Dangerous Drug Cartel."

64. "Veracruz se dejó en manos de los zetas, acusa Calderón" ("Calderón Accused (the former governor) of Leaving Veracruz in the Hands of Los Zetas"), October 15, 2011, available from *www.coatzadigital.net/2011/10/veracruz-se-dejo-en-manos-de-los-zetas.html*.

65. "Perfilan a embajada a Fidel Herrera" ("Fidel Herrera Is Touted for an Embassy"), *Reforma*, August 30, 2013; and "Piden no dar aval a Fidel" ("Asks that Fidel Doesn't Receive Endorsement"), *Reforma*, October 16, 2013.

66. William Booth, "Warrior in Drug Fight Soon Becomes a Victim," *Washington Post*, February 9, 2009.

67. Noemi Gutiérrez, "Afirman que por una canción mataron a Valentín" ("For a Song They Killed Valentín"), *El Universal*, November 27, 2006.

68. "Singer Shot, Killed While Hospitalized in Mexico, *U-T San Diego*, December 4, 2007.

69. Quoted in Jeremy Schwartz, "Musician Killings Highlight Unrelenting Violence in Mexico," *Banderas News*, December 2007.

70. Grant, "Mexico Violence: Fear and Intimidation."

71. "Secuestadores en México usan Google para seleccionar a víctimas" ("Kidnappers in Mexico Use Google to Choose Victims"), *International Business News*, February 15, 2011; "Secuestros Facilitados por Facebook" ("Kidnappings Facilitated by Facebook"), *Aunam Noticias: Agencia Estudiantil de Noticias Universarias*, October 5, 2012; Ildefonso Ortiz, "Gulf Cartel Member Sentenced for Recruiting Human Smugglers Online, *The Monitor*, July 15, 2013.

72. "Where is the Head of the Zetas Heriberto 'The Lazca' Lazcano?" March 18, 2012, available from *usopenborders.com/2012/03/where-is-the-head-of-the-zetas-heriberto-the-lazca-lazcano/*.

73. "'Los Zetas' reparten despensas en Tamaulipas" ("The Zetas Distribute Provisions in Tamaulipas"), *Proceso*, October 10, 2013.

74. "Invasion of the Body Snatchers."

75. *Ibid.*

76. Tim Padgett and Ioan Grillo, "Mexico Says 'The Executioner' is Dead—But Where's the Body?" *Time* magazine (World Ed.), October 10, 2012; and "Ponen en duda muerte de capo" ("Doubts Remain about the Capo's Death"), *Reforma*, September 6, 2013.

77. Arturo Rodríguez García, "Los Zetas, génesis de los conflictos en Topo Chico" ("Los Zetas, Genesis of Conflicts in Topo Chico"), *Proceso*, October 8, 2009.

78. "Ex militares sirven de sicarios a cárteles mexicanos" ("Ex military men serve as hitmen for Mexican Cartels"), *SeguRed.com*, July 25, 2006, available from *www.segured.com/index.php?od=9&link=7765*.

79. "Lanza Brandy de los 'Zetas'" ("Brandy 'Los Zetas' is Launched"), *RadiQuintana Roo,* March 23, 2009.

80. "El desempleo en México sube en septiembre de 2013" ("Mexican Unemployment Rose in September 2013"), *Informador. com.mx,* October 18, 2013.

81. "Economía informal 'arropa' a mexicanos" ("The Underground Economy Covers the Economy"), *CNNExpansión,* available from *www.cnnexapnsion.com/economia/2012/02/24/Mexico-menos-desempleo-mas-informales;* and *www.inegi.org.mx/sistemas/glosario/Default.aspx?ClvGlo=EHENOE&s=est&c=10842.*

82. Isabel Mayoral Jiménez,"Salario promedio, lejos de 6,000 pesos" ("Average Salary Far from 6,000 Pesos"), *CNNExpansión: Super Empresas 2012,* February 24, 2011.

83. Israel Rodríguez, "Bailey: 'mito urbano', que narcos traigan al país 29 mil mdd" ("Bailey: 'Urban Myth,' that Narcos Bring 29 Billion Dollars into Country"), *La Jornada,* September 27, 2013.

84. "'Zetas' usaron a El Recodo para lavar dinero en EU, revela FBI" ("The FBI Reveals that 'Zetas' Use El Recodo Band to Launder Money in the US"), Doris Gómora, *El Universal,* May 3, 2013.

85. Ware, "Los Zetas Called Mexico's Most Dangerous Drug Cartel."

86. "Falsos zetas se dedican a la extorsión" ("False Zetas Concentrate on Extortion"), *Consejo para la ley y los Derechos Humanos, A.C.,* October 25, 2007.

87. "Dan 'Zetas' narcoconsejo" ("Los Zetas Give Narco-Advice"), *Reforma,* May 4, 2008.

88. César Peralta González, "Ejecutan a falsos 'Zetas' en Reynosa, tenían un narcomensaje" (The Execution of False 'Zetas' in Reynosa Sends a Narco-Message"), *Milenio,* February 28, 2009.

89. "Sufren cuatro españoles plagio virtual en México" ("Four Spaniards Endure Virtual Kidnapping in Mexico"), *Reforma*, October 9, 2013; and "'Pensó que iban a pegarle un tiro'" ("'I Thought that Shots Would Be Fired'"), *Reforma*, October 12, 2013.

90. Quoted in Alfredo Corchado, "Mexico's Zetas Gang Buys Businesses along Border in Move to Increase Legitimacy," *Dallas Morning News*, December 7, 2009.

91. Jorge Volpi, "La Vida en México" ("The Life in Mexico"), *Reforma*, May 26, 2013.

92. Jason Buch, "Zetas Next Boss May be Worse than the One Just Killed," *My San Antonio.com*, October 10, 2012.

93. John P. Sullivan and Samuel Logan, "Los Zetas: Massacres, Assassinations and Infantry Tactics," *Homeland 1*, November 24, 2010.

94. Víctor Solís, "'Zetas' ganan terreno en el sureste de EU" ("'Zetas' Gain Ground in the U.S. Southeast"), *El Universal*, July 16, 2011.

95. Ximena Moretti, "Zetas utilizan mujeres como sicarios" ("Zetas use women as gunmen"), *Agora*, April 23, 2012.

96. "Cae operadora financiera del crimen organizado" ("Financial Operator of Organized Crime Captured"), *Diario de Xalapa*, October 28, 2011.

97. "Reclutan Zetas a mujeres" ("Los Zetas Recruit Women"), *El Norte*, March 27, 2009.

98. "Detienen el Norte de México a jefa de plaza de 'Los Zetas'" ("'Zeta' Female Plaza Boss Arrested in the North of Mexico"), *El Universal* (Caracas), September 11, 2011; and Rodolfo Santana, "Sostenía relación jefe de cártel con 'El Sureño'" ("Cartel Chief Involved in a Relationship with 'El Sureño'"), *Info 7*, September 13, 2011, available from *info7.mx/a/noticia/292226*.

99. Moretti, "Zetas utilizan mujeres como sicarios."

100. *Ibid.*

101. *Ibid.*

102. "Cae regidora de Victoria en casa Zeta" ("Member of Victoria City Council Arrested in Zeta House"), *Reforma*, August 26, 2013.

103. Moretti, "Zetas utilizan mujeres como sicarios."

104. "Se carean por una mujer" ("Confrontation over a Woman"), *Reforma*, October 14, 2013; and Krupskaia Alís, "México captura a 'la Ardilla', presunto jefe regional de los Zetas" ("Mexico Captures 'la Ardilla,' presumed regional chief of Los Zetas") *CNN Español*, October 8, 2012.

105. Luis Prados, "Lucha a muerte en los Zetas" ("Fight to the Death in the Zetas"), *El Pais* (International), September 16, 2012; Henry Orrego, "Mexico captures Zetas cartel Capo 'El Taliban': navy," Agence France Presse, September 27, 2012.

106. Quoted in Ginger Thompson, "U.S. Agencies Infiltrating Drug Cartels Across Mexico," *New York Times*, October 24, 2011.

107. Federal Bureau of Investigations, "Los Zetas Expanding Reach into Southeast and Midwest United States," *FBI Intelligence Bulletin*, October 2, 2008.

108. Lynn Brezosky, "Lake Killing Blamed on Blunder," October 13, 2010, available from *www.mysanantonio.com*; and *www.dailymail.co.uk/news/article-2214848/David-Hartley-death-Mexican-cartel-leader-known-Commander-Squirrel arrested.html#ixzz2TfTzPAsE*.

109. "The Black Kiss: Zetas Groomed Texas Teens as Sicarios at 13," *Borderland Beat*, July 5, 2012.

110 "3 people Associated with U.S. Consulate Killed in Mexico," *CNN World*, March 15, 2010.

111. Esprit Smith, "Drug Cartel Leader Captured in Northern Mexico," *CNNWorld*, June 10, 2010.

112. "Matan en País a más estadounidenses" ("More Americans Killed in the Country"), *Reforma*, May 19, 2013. According to the U.S. State Department, the number of U.S. citizens murdered in Mexico dropped from 113 in 2011 and 71 in 2012. See Jared Taylor, "Tamaulipas' Murder Rate up 90 Percent, Kidnappings Double, U.S. State Department Says," *The Monitor*, July 13, 2013.

113. "Zetas Racing Horses Will Be Auctioned Off," *Fox News Latino*, October 9, 2012.

114. Dane Schiller, "Los Zetas entrenan en un rancho que mantienen en Texas, según el FBI" ("The Zetas Train in a Ranch They Maintain in Texas, according to the FBI") *Houston Chronicle* (Spanish edition), May 27, 2009.

115. "Armamento de 'Los Zetas' se compra en EU, dice fundador del grupo crimina," ("Criminal Group's Founder Says that 'Los Zetas' Buy Weapons in the U.S."), *CNNMéxico*, July 5, 2011.

116. Ildefonso Ortiz, "Slain Singer Chuy Quintanilla Gained Fame for Drug War Ballads," *The Monitor* (McAllen, Texas), April 26, 2013; and "Suena en la red el corrido de El Hummer" ("One Hears on the Network a Ballad to El Hummer"), *El Universal*, November 8, 2008.

117. Richard Fausset, "A Kidnapping Mystery in Mexico City," *Los Angeles Times*, May 31, 2013.

118. "Conocía PGR tráfico de datos" ("The PGR Knew about the Traffic in Data"), *Reforma*, June 4, 2013.

119. Santiago Wills and Esteban Roman, "What Elba Esther Gordillo's Arrest Means for Mexico's Other Power Players," *ABC News*, March 1, 2013.

120. Leonor Flores, "SHCP detecta nuevas formas de lavar dinero" ("SHCP Detects New Forms to Launder Money"), *El Economista*, January 19, 2012.

121. For an analysis of the Ley para la Prevención e Identificación de Operaciones con Recursos de Procedencia Ilícita (Law for the Prevention and Identification of Operations with Resources from Illicit Activities), see David Henry Foulkes, "Con la ley

de prevención de lavado de dinero todos los contadores estarán regulados" ("All Accountants Will be Regulated Under the New Anti-Money Laundering Law"), *Diario Jurídico México*, January 3, 2013.

122. "El Recodo Was Paid $250,000 to Play at Parties for Los Zetas," *Borderland Beat*, May 7, 2013; Gómora, "'Zetas' usaron a El Recodo para lavar dinero en EU, revela FBI" ("'Zetas' Use El Recodo Band to Launder Money in the US, the FBI Reveals"), *El Universal*, May 3, 2013.

123. Adriana Gómez Licón, "Drones Help Fight Mexico Drug Cartels," *El Paso Times*, March 17, 2011.

124. Christopher Wilson, "Todos Somos Nuevo Laredo? How Mexico's PRI Can Make Nuevo Laredo into Juárez" Washington, DC: Mexico Institute, Woodrow Wilson Center, August 7, 2013.

125. Rosario Mosso Castro and Christian Torres Cruz, "The Growing Use of Juvenile Hit Men by Mexican Drug Lords," *Mexidata.Info*, June 3, 2013.

126. Adriana Varillas, "Reporta Pemex aumentó en robo de gasolina y diesel" ("Pemex Reports an Increase in the Theft of Gasoline and Diesel"), *El Universal*, June 6, 2013.

127. Nathaniel Parish Flannery, "Investor Insight: Why The Time May Be Right For Energy Reform In Mexico," *Forbes*, October 28, 2013.

128. U.S. Department of the Treasury, Office of Foreign Assets Control, "Treasury Targets Los Zetas Linked Oil Services Company," August 2012.

129. A highly regarded Mexican intellectual, university administrator, and former federal deputy makes this point splendidly. See Agustín Basave Benítez, *Mexicanidad y esquizofrenia: Los dos rostros del mexiJano* (*The Mexican Identify: The Two Faces of the Mexican*), Mexico City, Mexico: Editorial Océano, 2010.

APPENDIX I

EVOLUTION OF THE GULF CARTEL
AND LOS ZETAS

Date	Event	Consequence
1992–95	Jorge Eduardo "El Coss" Sánchez was a local police officer in Matamoros, the base of the Gulf Cartel	He learned the drug business at the grassroots level
January 14, 1996	Gulf capo Juan Ábrego García, nephew of infamous bootlegger Don Juan Nepomuceno Guerra (1915–2001), captured outside of Monterrey	Even though a minor player, El Coss befriended Osiel "The Friend Killer" Cárdenas Guillén and seized the reins of the cartel
March 14, 2003	Army captured Osiel Cárdenas Guillén, head of the Gulf Cartel	Top leader captured
March 14, 2003	Jorge Eduardo "El Coss" Costilla Sánchez assumed leadership	New leader assumes leadership
2004–10	A troika evolved that was composed of El Coss, Antonio "Tony Tormenta" Cárdenas Guillén, and Zeta leader Heriberto"Z-3" Lazcano Lazcano	Even as the Gulf Cartel repelled efforts by El Chapo and his allies to invade the north, frictions multiplied among troika members
2005	Friction increased as Los Zetas indulged in grotesque cruelty and formed situational alliances with the Beltrán Leyva Organization (BLO), a rival cartel	The brutality was at odds with the profit orientation of the Gulf and Sinaloa Cartels
January 20, 2007	Mexico extradited Osiel Cárdenas to the United States	Cooperation with U.S. authorities
February 24, 2010	A federal judge sentenced Osiel Cárdenas to 25 years in prison; he provided information to U.S. agents in exchange for a lighter term*	Zeta leader believed that Osiel had disclosed information about their tactics, leadership, and organization
January 18, 2010	El Coss ordered Samuel "Metro 3" Flores Borrego to kill Sergio "Concord" Peña Mendoza, a confidant of "El 40"	Animus evolves to warfare between the Gulf Cartel and Los Zetas

71

November 5, 2010	Navy killed Tony Tormenta after a fierce gun battle in Matamoros	Three of his bodyguards, known as "Los Escorpianos," were also killed, as were two members of the navy's Special Forces and a reporter
November 5, 2010	Osiel's brother Mario Cárdenas Guillén reluctantly assumed leadership	Another brother of Osiel comes to the fore
March 2011	Mario Cárdenas Guillén relinquished the reins of the cartel	Changing of the guard in the Gulf Cartel
March 2011	Rafael "El Junior" Cárdenas Vela, nephew of Osiel and former head of Matamoros plaza, took over	New leader takes over
September 2, 2011	Tortured and bound bodies of Flores Borrego and Eloy Lerma García, a high ranking local police officer, are found 13 miles south of Reynosa	Los Zetas got revenge for the death of Metro 3
October 11, 2011	Body of César "Gama" Dávila García, Tony Tormenta's personal accountant was found in an abandoned house in Reynosa	Another event in intramural battle for control of the cartel
October 20, 2011	ICE captured Rafael "El Junior" Cárdenas Vela in Port Isabel, Texas; wearing pink shorts and loafers, he was heading toward his South Padre Island residence	El Junior's testimony helped convict Juan Roberto Rincón-Rincón, the Gulf's plaza boss in Rio Bravo, Tamaulipas; Cárdenas Vela was living in the United States to escape revenge by Gulf Cartel rivals
October 26, 2011	U.S. Border Patrol arrested Juan Roberto "Comandante Primo" Rincón-Rincón in Santa Maria, Texas	Former regional Gulf Cartel commander who said that one smuggler working for him moved 500 kilograms of cocaine into the United States each week

October 26, 2011	U.S. Border Patrol arrested José Luis "Comandante Wicho" Zuñiga Hernández in Santa Maria, Texas, after he fled a gun battle in Río Bravo, Mexico	Comandante Wicho was arrested along with Rincón as the men tried to escape rivals in the Gulf Cartel, Los Rojas; indicted in late-September 2012, along with Luis Iván "Machín" Nino Duenes and Armando "Comandante Mando" Arizmendi Hernández, for conspiracy to traffic drugs
October 26, 2011	Navy apprehended Carmen del Consuelo "Claudia" Sáenz Márquez in Córdoba, Veracruz	Major financial operator in the states of Hidalgo, Oaxaca, Tabasco, Quintana Roo, and Veracruz
December 12, 2011	Navy captured Raúl Lucio "El Lucky" Hernández Lechuga	Key Zeta regional boss in Veracruz, Puebla, and southern Mexico
May 9, 2012	Gilberto Lerma Plata, former Tamaulipas police chief and cousin of ex-governor Manuel Cavazos Lerma and current senator, arrested in McAllen for smuggling drugs into south Texas for the Gulf Cartel	Confessed to charges and sentenced
June 9, 2012	Fernando Herrera Zurita, who used aliases, including Erick "El Orejón" Cárdenas Guíza, captured by marines on Veracruz-Xalapa highway; PGR said suspect coordinated drug and arms traffic from Guatemala to Tamaulipas and Nuevo León	The elimination of a skilled operator
July 26, 2012	Marines detailed Mauricio Guizar Cárdenas in DF; alleged leader of Los etas in Chiapas, Campeche, Quintana Roo, and Veracruz	Fall of an important regional leader
September 3, 2012	Marines captured Mario Cárdenas Guillén in Altamira, Tamaulipas	Another setback to the cartel's ebbing strength
September 7, 2012	Marines apprehended Juan Carlos "El Peluches" Morales; presumed Zeta chief in Piedras Negras, Coahuila	The fall of an ally of Lazcano

September 11, 2012	Marines arrested Juan Gabriel "Sierra" Montes Sermeño in Guadalajara	Leader of Gulf Cartel's strike team known as the Kalimanes; captured with bodyguard Eusebio Horta Arguellos
September 12, 2012	Marines arrested "El Coss" in Tampico	Cartel weakened even more; Homero Cárdenas,** a family member, became the leader of the Los Rojas (pro–Cárdenas Guillén) wing of the Gulf Cartel; Mario Armando "El Pelón"/"X-20" Ramírez Treviño took charge of Los Metros" (pro- Coss) faction of the Gulf Cartel. He controled Reynosa through a wrestler, José Alejandro "El Simple" Leal, but often stayed a few miles away in Río Bravo, Tamaulipas
September 26, 2012	Marines arrested Iván "El Talibán" Velázquez Caballero in San Luis Potosí	Chief of Zeta faction opposing "El 40" as power-hungry and a "Judas"; alleged that he defected to the Gulf Cartel to which he previously belonged; extradited to the U.S. on November 23, 2013
October 5, 2012	Marines and state authorities appended Carlos "El Carlangas" Carmona; led a Zeta group in southern Veracruz municipalities of Ángel R. Cabada, Lerdo de Tejada, Cosamaloapan, Rodríguez Clara, Isla, San Andrés Tuxtla, Santiago Tuxtla, Catemaco, and Coatzacoalcos; also arrested were 2 male and 2 female Zetas, who carried high-powered weapons and drugs.	A success for navy/marines
October 6, 2012	Marines captured Salvador "La Ardilla" Martínez Escobedo in Nuevo Laredo	Enemy of "El 40" and key leader in Coahuila, Tamaulipas, and Nuevo León

October 7, 2012	Marines captured Zeta leader Heriberto Lazcano in Progreso, Coahuila	Comrades stole his body from the funeral home; fingerprint matches and DNA tests supposedly confirmed his identity, even though the DEA has expressed doubts about his death
November 2012	U.S. Homeland Security agents apprehended gun traffickers Juan Ricardo Martínez Cárdenas and Daniel Blanco Avila in Roma, Texas	To avoid the Gulf Cartel, these men smuggled guns from Miguel Alemán, Tamaulipas, to Roma, Texas, before bringing them back to Miguel Alemán; Los Zetas paid them $1,200 every 2 weeks
December 2012	Marines arrested Francisco Dair Montalvo Recio in Nuevo Laredo. "Rocky," was the accountant in Nuevo Laredo and was found with upwards of $5 million in pesos and dollars. Also captured were three accomplices.	Montalvo Recio supplied naval intelligence with invaluable information about the movements of Zeta chief "El 40, who was taken into custody on July 15, 2013, near Nuevo Laredo
January 15, 2013	Authorities found the corpse of Héctor "Metro 4" Delgado	Ruthless enforcer for Gulf Cartel
January 24, 2013	Jose Luis "El Wicho" Zuñiga Hernández sentenced to 7 years in prison	Put behind bars a Gulf Cartel operative captured by the U.S. Border Patrol in October 2011 and known for arms smuggling, kidnapping, and immigration violations
March 10, 2013	Armed forces killed Miguel "El Gringo" Villarreal in Reynosa	He challenged El Pelón Ramírez Treviño for leadership of the Gulf Cartel
May 8, 2013	Marines apprehended Alfonso Zamudio Quijada, the presumed accountant of Los Zetas in Monclova, Coahuila	A financial blow inasmuch as the suspect was in possession of an AK-47 assault rifle, ammunition, some $300,000 in cash, and 500 plastic bags containing a white, powdery substance resembling cocaine

July 15, 2013	Marines captured El 40 Treviño Morales near Nuevo Laredo	Severe blow to Los Zetas, which lost its most sadistic chief
August 17, 2013	Army captured El Pelón Ramírez Treviño in Río Bravo	Will require El Chapo[***] to exert more pressure on the factions of the Gulf Cartel to maintain their fragile unity
November 21, 2013	State and navy tactical groups captured Jorge "El Ruso" Uvaldo del Fierro Varela, along with 3 other Zetas and 13 Federal Police, who allegedly protected them in Saltillo where El Ruso was a key operative	A setback to Los Zetas in a Coahuila, a northern state where they retain a significant presence
April 2014	Authorities captured El Simple—a move that sparked violence in Reynosa, which took the life of a Federal Police Officer (April 1); 30 killed in gun battles in Tampico (Easter Week)	The Reynosa firefight included Los Metros and "Los Ciclones," who were investigating the alleged death of Homero Cárdenas Guillén; internecine fighting surges in Gulf

[*] The 7 years that he had served in Mexico reduced his 25-year term, which could be shortened even more for continued cooperation.

[**] Homero Cárdenas, believed to be a cousin of Mario Cárdenas Guillén, is reportedly in line to take over the reins of the cartel; other allies of "El Pelón" included "Metro 4," Alfonso "Metro 7" Flores Borrego, and ex-Zeta Cruz Galindo Mellado, who realigned with the Gulf Cartel.

[***] El Chapo, who sided with Los Metros, reportedly dispatched members of the Guadalajara-based Jalisco New Generation Cartel put an end to the intramural feuding; the drug lord was captured on February 22, 2014.

Sources: "Mexico Zeta Drug Gang Leader "El Lucky" Arrested," *BBC News Latin America and Caribbean,* December 12, 2011. This appendix relies heavily on articles by the border's top criminal reporter, Ildefonso Oritz, at *The Monitor* (McAllen, TX); "Gulf Cartel Commander Asks for Jury Trial in Brownsville," September 19, 2012; "Siempre a salto de mata" ("Always in Dribs and Drabs"), *Reforma,* October 9, 2012; "Detainee: Zetas Smuggle Guns into US to Avoid Gulf Cartel" *The Monitor,* November 30, 2012; "Few Details Known about Quiet Fall of Feared Gulf Cartel Kingpin," January 27, 2013; "Gulf Cartel, Zetas Mark 3rd Anniversary of Bloody Rivalry," February 6, 2013; Jared Taylor, "Former Tamps: Police Chief, Cousin of Ex-Governor, Admits to Gulf Cartel Ties," *The Monitor,* March 3, 2013; Doris Gómera, "Ex-Comandante admite que fue cómplice del cártel del golfo" ("Ex-Commander Admits that He Was an Accomplice of the Gulf Cartel"), *El Universal,* March 5, 2013; Havana Pura, "Accountant El Rocky Snithced on Z-40," *Borderland Beat,* July 27, 2013; Mark Reagan, "'El Wicho,' Other Cartel Figures Make Court Appearance," *Brownsville Herald,* October 18, 2013; "Capturan a zeta con 13 federales; era jefe de plaza en Saltillo" ("Zeta Plaza Boss in Saltillo Captured with 13 Federal Police"), *Excélsior,* November 24, 2013; and "Los Golpes al crimen" ("Blows against Crime"), *Reforma,* December 2013. A version of this appendix appears in George W. Grayson, *The Cartels: The Story of Mexico's Most Dangerous Criminal Organizations and Their Impact on U.S. Security* (Santa Barbara, CA: Praeger, 2014).

APPENDIX II

SADISTIC PERSONALITY DISORDER CRITERIA

- Maladaptive patterns of motivated behavior, usually evident for at least several years.
- Enduring, pervasive, maladaptive patterns of behavior which are usually recognized before or during adolescence.
- It is long-standing and its onset can be traced to adolescence or early adulthood but is not due to drugs (or abuse of medication) or to a medical condition such as a head injury.
- The behavior pattern is inflexible across all personal and social situations and significantly impairs social or occupational functioning.
- Has used physical cruelty or violence for the purpose of establishing dominance in a relationship (not merely to achieve some noninterpersonal goal, such as striking someone in order to rob him or her).
- Humiliates or demeans people in the presence of others.
- Has treated or disciplined someone under his or her control usually harshly, e.g., a child, student, prisoner, or patient.
- Is amused by, or takes pleasure in, the psychological or physical suffering of others (including animals).
- Has lied for the purpose of harming or inflicting pain on others (including animals).
- Gets other people to do what he wants by frightening them through intimidation or even terror.

- Restricts the autonomy of people with whom he or she has a close relationship, e.g., will not let spouse leave the house unaccompanied or permit teenage daughter to attend social functions.
- Is fascinated by violence, weapons, martial arts, injury, or torture.

Source: "Sadistic Personality Disorder Criteria," PsychNet-UK, March 2013.

APPENDIX III

CRIMINAL ACTIVITIES OF LOS ZETAS

Illegal Activities	Examples
Drug Smuggling	Marijuana and some cocaine, and methamphetamines, and heroin.
Extortion	Even when behind bars, Los Zetas, who have detailed information about a family, demand money to prevent the kidnapping of a loved one.
Kidnapping	Illegal immigrants passing through Mexico; cells in most plazas dedicated to this crime.
Human Smuggling	The Mexican Human Rights Commission reported that in the first 6 months of 2009, 9,758 illegal aliens crossing into Mexico were kidnapped and 13 assassinated. Of these victims, 91 reported complicity by "agents of the state," usually functionaries of the Mexican Migration Institute (INM).
Contraband	U.S. officials and representatives of film studios and software manufacturers claim that Los Zetas and other cartels take a big cut out of the hundreds of millions of dollars in bootleg disks sold each year in Mexico.
Selling Babies	Los Zetas impregnate captured Central American immigrants whose babies they sell, often in Guatemala.
Petroleum Rustling	PEMEX suffered 1,267 thefts in 3 years, at a cost of 5,125 million pesos (U.S.$427 million) between 2007 and mid-2012. These quantities are creating a virtual "Parallel PEMEX."

Sale of Body Parts	A Zeta commander allegedly kidnapped 100 illegal Guatemalans working in a shirt factory in Coatzacoalcos, Veracruz: According to an escapee, the women were turned into prostitutes; the older men were forced to become lookouts or small-time drug sellers; and the bodies of some of the healthier young men were harvested for kidneys and other body parts.
Money Laundering	Invested in quarter horses in the United States; however, unlike business-oriented cartels, they have not purchased real estate and other assets in Mexico.
Prostitution	Cuban prostitutes in Cancún; "buying" Central American women from an Immigrant smuggler and exploiting them as prostitutes in Reynosa bars and hotels.
Selling the Right to Cross its Territory (Derecho de Piso)	Threatened gas producers in Burgos basin in Tamaulipas and Nuevo León with death if they did not pay for the right to operate.
Murder for Hire	Los Zetas allegedly paid Eduardo González "El Lalito" Trejo (or Eduardo Trejo Ponce), 40,000 pesos to murder Víctor Hugo Moneda, ex-commander of the DF's Judicial Police.
Selling Protection	To the BLO and to Cuban gangs in Cancún.
Theft of Automobiles and Trucks	Especially along the borders of Tamaulipas and Nuevo León with the United States
Paying Small Farmers to Grow Poppies and Move Contraband into Mexico	Notably in Guatemala.

Arson	Just after Christmas 2010, in a battle with the Sinaloa Cartel, Zetas set fire to houses in Tierras Coloradas, Durango, leaving homeless 150 Tepehuan Indians who speak Spanish as a second language and have no electricity or running water; the victims had already fled into the woods, sleeping under trees or hiding in caves after a raid by feared drug gangs on December 26; residents suffered cold winter weather, and the crops of farmers who refused to cooperate were burned.
Street Blocks, Which Give Them Access to Their Targets	Notably in Monterrey and Reynosa where they use ponchallantas (small, sharp metallic stars that blow out tires).
Public Works Concessions	Mayors, especially in small municipalities, are coerced into awarding construction contracts to Los Zetas, who turn over the project to a contractor for 35 percent of the payment for the job.
Masquerade as Police or Military Officials	Catches targets off guard; helps them gain entrance to jails, rehabilitation centers, and other venues where they have a mission.
Car Bombings	May constitute "tipping point" between criminality and terrorism, according to Group Savant CEO Gary J. Hale.
Tunneling	The Sinaloa Cartel has access to engineers, contractors, and other experts to excavate sophisticated, cross-border tunnels; however, Los Zetas have plotted the digging of shorter passageways such as the one that facilitated the escape of 129 inmates from a prison (Cereso) in Piedras Negras, Coahuila, in mid-September 2012.

Sources: William & Mary outstanding law student Lindsey C. Nicolai; and Lisa J. Campbell, "Los Zetas," in Robert J. Bunker, ed., *Narcos Over the Border: Gangs, Cartels and Mercenaries*, New York: Routledge, 2011, pp. 70-71; "Los Zetas, tras ejecución del comandante Monteda"("Los Zetas after the Execution of Commander Monteda"), *Milenio.com*, March 18, 2009; Noé Cruz Serrano, "Robo financió un 'Pemex paralelo'" ("Robberies Finance a Parallel PEMEX"), *El Universal*, July 31, 2009; "Cancún: las cubanas secuestradas, en red de prostitución de los Zetas" ("Cancún: Kidnapped Cuban Women Form Los Zetas Prostitution Network"), *Cubadebate,* September 17, 2009; Alfredo Corchado, "Mexico's Zetas Gang Buys Businesses along Border in Move to Increase Legitimacy," *Dallas Morning News*, December 7, 2009; "Cobran zetas 'derecho de piso' a gaseras en el norte del pais" ("Zetas Charge 'Crossing Fees' to Gas Producers in the North of the Country"), *Noticias Durango Hoy*, February 16, 2011; Antonio Baranda, "Perfeccionan reos táctica de extorsión" ("Criminals Perfect Extortion Tactics"), *Reforma.com*, June 1, 2010; Mica Rosenberg, "Mexico's Refugees: a Hidden Cost of Drugs War," *Reuters*, February 17, 2011; "'Zetas' incendian pueblo en Durango" ("'Zetas' Burn Village in Durango"), *El Economista*, February 18, 2011; Samuel Logan, "Networked Intelligence: Southern Pulse," May 10, 2011, "Petroleum Rustling," Verónica Sánchez, "Registrar desde 2009 liga entre INM-narco" ("Recognized since 2009 a Link between INM and Narcos"), *Reforma*, May 11, 2011; William Booth, "Mexico's Thriving Piracy Business Funds Cartels," *The Washington Post*, May 30, 2011; Anne-Marie O'Connor, "Mexico's 'Inferno' of Exploitation," *The Washington Post*, July 28, 2011; Chivis Martinez, "Piedras Negras: Zetas Likely Behind New Prison Break," *Border Beat*, September 19, 2012; "Entra crimen obra pública" ("Crime Enters Public Works"), *Reforma*, October 14, 2012; and Alberto Tinoco Guadarrama, "La violencia and inseguridad en Tamaulipas" ("The Violence and Insecurity in Tamaulipas"), *Noticieros Televisa*, January 22, 2013; Raúl Benítez Manaut, "Organized Crime as the Highest Threat to Mexican National Security and Democracy," Tony Payan, Kathleen Staudt, and Z. Anthony Kruszewski, eds., *A War That Can't Be Won: Binational Perspectives on the War on Drugs*, Tucson, AZ: University of Arizona Press, 2013, pp. 149-173.

This appendix is a revised and updated version of "Table 4: Diversification of Los Zetas' Criminal Activities," in George W. Grayson and Samuel Logan, *The Executioner's Men: Los Zetas, Rogue Soldiers, Criminal Entrepreneurs, and the Shadow State They Created*, New Brunswick, NJ: Transaction Publishers, 2012, pp. 51-53.

APPENDIX IV

COMPARISON OF MURDERS IN TWIN CITIES ALONG THE U.S.-MEXICAN BORDER

U.S. Cities	Murders per 100,000 people	Total Murders	Mexican Cities	Murders *(Homicidios Dolosos)* per 100,000 people	Total Murders
Brownsville	1.66 (2012) 0.55 (2011) 3.96 (2010) 2.3 (2009) 2.2 (2008)	3 (2012) 1 (2011) 7 (2010) 4 (2009) 4 (2008)	Matamoros	N/A (2012) 17.03 (2011) N/A (2010) N/A (2009) N/A (2008)	N/A (2012) 72 (Jan-Sep 2011) N/A (2010) N/A (2009) N/A (2008)
El Paso	3.39 (2012) 2.40 (2011) .77 (2010) 2.00 (2009) 2.77 (2008)	22 (2012) 16 (2011) 5 (2010) 13 (2009) 18 (2008)	Ciudad Juárez	49.6 (2012) 48.3 (2011) 223 (2010) 189 (2009) 130 (2008)	750 (2012) 1,976 (2011) 3,622 (2010) 2,643 (2009) 1,587 (2008)
Laredo	4.09 (2012) 4.60 (2011) 3.99 (2010) 8.43 (2009) 4.44 (2008)	10 (2012) 11 (2011) 9 (2010) 19 (2009) 10 (2008)	Nuevo Laredo	72.85 (2012) N/A (2011) N/A (2010) N/A (2009) N/A (2008)	288 (2012) 144 (Jan 2011) N/A (2010) N/A (2009) N/A (2008)
Mc Allen	.07 (2012) 3.00 (2011) 3.64 (2010) 2.91 (2009) 6.74 (2008)	1 (2012) 4 (2011) 5 (2010) 4 (2009) 9 (2008)	Reynosa	N/A (2012) 9.68. (2011) 41.1 (2010) N/A (2009) N/A (2008)	N/A (2012) 51 (Jan 2011) 217 (2010) N/A (2009) N/A (2008)
San Diego	.04 (2012) .03 (2011) .02 (2010) .03 (2009) .04 (2008)	47 (2012) 38 (2011) 29 (2010) 41 (2009) 55 (2008)	Tijuana	15.58 (Jan-June 2013) 20.29 (2012) 36.05 (2011) 52.50 (2010) 40.76 (2009) 51.81 (2008)	278 (Jan-June 2013) 362 (2012) 469 (2011) 826 (2010) 664 (2009) 844 (2008)

Sources: Sean Gaffney, "Juárez, la ciudad más violenta del mundo" (Juárez, The Most Violent City in the World"), El Economista, August 26, 2009; "McAllen: One of the Most Secure Places to Live, Study Finds," The Monitor, December 23, 2009; SIA Informe: "Ciudades latinoamericanas entre los más violentas del mundo ("Latin American Cities among the Most Violent in the World"), February 10,

2011; McAllen Police Department, Crime Records Office, City of McAllen Crime Report 2010, 2011, 2012: Laredo Police Department, 2010 Annual Report; San Diego Historical Crime Rates per 1,000 Population, 1950-2010, available from *www.sandiego.gov/police/pdf/crimerates.pdf,* "El Paso See Double Digit Decrease in Murders, Other Major Crimes," KVIA.com, November 5, 2010; City of San Diego, San Diego Police Department, "Actual Crimes, 1950-2012"; "Crime rate in Brownsville, Texas (TX): murders, rapes, robberies, assaults, burglaries, thefts, auto thefts, arson, law enforcement employees, police officers, crime map," *www. city-data.com/crime/crime-Brownsville-Texas.html#ixzz2TxICvnOX*; and Maria Garcia "Juárez Murder Rate Decreases 45% in 2011," ABC7 (El Paso), based on figures provides by Molly Molloy, Librarian, New Mexico State University (Las Cruces); Alidad Vassigh, "Latin American cities are the most dangerous in the world," City Mayors Security 28, October 12, 2012, available from *www.citymayors.com/ security/latin-american-murder-cities.html*; Procuraduría General de la República, "Total Fallecimientos por presunta rivalad delincuencial: Enero-Septiembre 2011" ("Total Deaths from Presumed Criminal Rivalries, January-September 2011), December 2012; Luis Gerardo Andrade, "Baja homicidios un 23% durante 2012 en Tijuana" ("Homicides Fall 23% during 2012 in Tijuana"), Frontera.com, January 1, 2013; and Jared Taylor, "Tamaulipas' Murder Rate up 90 Percent, Kidnappings Double, U.S. State Department Says," The Monitor, July 13, 2012.

APPENDIX V

MOST MURDER-RIDDEN CITIES IN THE AMERICAS (NUMBER OF MURDERS PER 100,000 INHABITANTS PER ANNUM)

Rank	City	Country	Population	Murder Rate (2011)	Murder Rate (2010)
1	San Pedro Sula	Honduras	719,447	158.87	125 (2010)
2	Ciudad Juárez	Mexico	1,335,890	147.77	229 (2010)
3	Maceió	Brazil	1,156,278	135.26	n/a
4	Acapulco	Mexico	804,412	127.92	51.4 (2010)
5	Capital District	Honduras	1,126,534	99.69	108 (2010)
6	Caracas	Venezuela	3,205,463	98.71	118 (2010)
7	Torreón (metropolitan)	Mexico	1,128,152	87.75	68.4 (2010)
8	Chihuahua	Mexico	831,693	82.96	113 (2010)
9	Durango	Mexico	593,389	79.88	78.3 (2010)
10	Belém	Brazil	2,100,319	78.04	n/a
11	Cali	Colombia	2,207,994	77.90	87.4 (2010)
12	Guatemala City	Guatemala	3,014,060	74.58	106 (2010)
13	Culiacán	Mexico	871,620	74.46	87.8 (2010)
14	Medellín	Colombia	2,309,446	70.32	87.4 (2010)
15	Mazatlán	Mexico	445,343	68.94	88.1 (2010)
16	Tepic (metropolitan)	Mexico	439,362	68.05	79.9 (2010)
17	Vitória	Brazil	1,685,384	67.82	76.1 (2010)
18	Veracruz	Mexico	697,414	59.94	n/a
19	Ciudad Guayana	Venezuela	940,477	58.91	68.8 (2010)
20	San Salvador	El Salvador	2,290,790	58.63	82.9 (2010)
21	New Orleans	USA	343,829	57.88	69 (2009)
22	Salvador	Brazil	3,574,804	56.98	n/a
23	Cúcuta	Colombia	597,385	56.08	56.1 (2010)

| 24 | Barquisemeto | Venezuela | 1,120,718 | 55.41 | n/a |
| 25 | San Juan | Puerto Rico | 427,789 | 52.60 | n/a |

Source: Alidad Vassigh, "Latin American cities are the most dangerous in the world," *City Mayors Security* 28, October 12, 2012, available from *www.citymayors.com/security/latin-american-murder cities.html.*